Gross Mazes Book

Wind your way through hours of
twisted turns, sick shortcuts, and disgusting detours!

Beth L. Blair

D1303028

Adams Media
Avon, Massachusetts

EDITORIAL
Publishing Director: Gary M. Krebs
Associate Managing Editor: Laura M. Daly
Associate Copy Chief: Brett Palana-Shanahan
Acquisitions Editor: Kate Burgo
Associate Production Editor: Casey Ebert

PRODUCTION
Director of Manufacturing: Susan Beale
Associate Director of Production: Michelle Roy Kelly
Series Designers: Colleen Cunningham, Erin Ring
Layout and Graphics: Colleen Cunningham,
    Sorae Lee, Jennifer Oliveira
Cover Layout: Paul Beatrice, Erick DaCosta,
    Matt LeBlanc

An Everything® Series Book.
Everything® and everything.com® are registered trademarks of F+W Publications, Inc.

Published by Adams Media, an F+W Publications Company
57 Littlefield Street, Avon, MA 02322. U.S.A.
www.adamsmedia.com

ISBN 10: 1-59337-616-2
ISBN 13: 978-1-59337-616-1
Printed in the United States of America.

J I H G F E D C B

Library of Congress Cataloging-in-Publication Data
available from publisher.

This publication is designed to provide accurate and authoritative information with regard to the subject matter covered. It is sold with the understanding that the publisher is not engaged in rendering legal, accounting, or other professional advice. If legal advice or other expert assistance is required, the services of a competent professional person
should be sought.

—From a *Declaration of Principles* jointly adopted by a Committee of the
American Bar Association and a Committee of Publishers and Associations

Many of the designations used by manufacturers and sellers to distinguish their products are claimed as trademarks.
When those designations appear in this book and Adams Media was aware of a trademark claim, the designations have
been printed with initial capital letters.

Cover and interior illustrations by Kurt Dolber.
Puzzles by Beth L. Blair.

This book is available at quantity discounts for bulk purchases.
For information, call 1-800-289-0963.

See the entire Everything® series at *www.everything.com*.

Contents

Introduction

Let's Get Gross!

OK, so I had to write a book about gross. Where to start?

Well, the great thing about gross is that it comes in all sizes and shapes! From the tiniest dust mite living in your mattress to the largest pile of hippo poop, there are enough different kinds of gross to keep everyone yelling "Eeeeew!" There's the mysterious gross you find on the bottom of your shoe, and the inedible gross you might get served for dinner. And don't forget the truly smelly gross or the disgustingly dirty gross, either. In fact, there's so much gross both on and around us, it was hard to decide just what to include.

But wait, this is also a maze book! So a lot of the gross things also had to be twisty (like sewer pipes), or slithery (like snake skin), or curly (like noodles out the nose). At least they had to make interesting patterns to wander through, like blobs on the beach, floating poops, or farting termites.

Then there's gross stuff that's just too interesting to get left out, like replacement body parts, disgusting jobs, and recipes that call for ground up mummies. (I didn't make that up, really!)

So, after much researching, writing, drawing (and erasing), and a whole ton of "YUCK!"ing, here it is—a great big, gooey, slimy, wiggling, and definitely bug-covered collection of gross mazes. You'll see that there really is some kind of gross for everyone!

Your smelly friend,*

Beth L. Blair

*Hey, don't wrinkle up your nose like that.
You're smelly, too. We ALL are! Isn't that gross?

One more thing: Unless the directions say "go over and under," you should not cross any of the solid lines as you solve the mazes. There are lots of different colors and shades of colors that swirl through the pictures. It's OK to have your path go over those. But no taking shortcuts over the solid lines, OK?

Tattoo Black & Blue

Every tattoo is the same in one way—somehow, a sharp object is used to stick ink into the skin.

START

The modern tattoo machine pushes an ink-filled needle in and out of the skin up to 3,000 times a minute. OUCH!

As you poke your way through this tattoo, find the bird, skull, rose, snake, and sword!

END

Icky Itchy Ivy

You start out with a little itch. Then your skin gets pink and bubbly. All of a sudden you're covered with oozing sores and look like a mutant red alligator—and you just *can't* stop scratching. Sounds like a case of poison ivy! It's the oil "urushiol" that gives poison ivy its punch. This plant chemical is so powerful that just a tiny amount, about the size of a pinhead, could make 500 people itchy!

Find your way around the blisters and the puddles of Calamine lotion from where you **START** itching to where you **END** up scratching.

GROSS, BUT TRUE!

You'd better watch out if someone accidentally burns poison ivy in his or her yard. If you breath smoke that has droplets of urushiol oil in it, you can get a poison ivy rash right up your nose and down into your lungs!

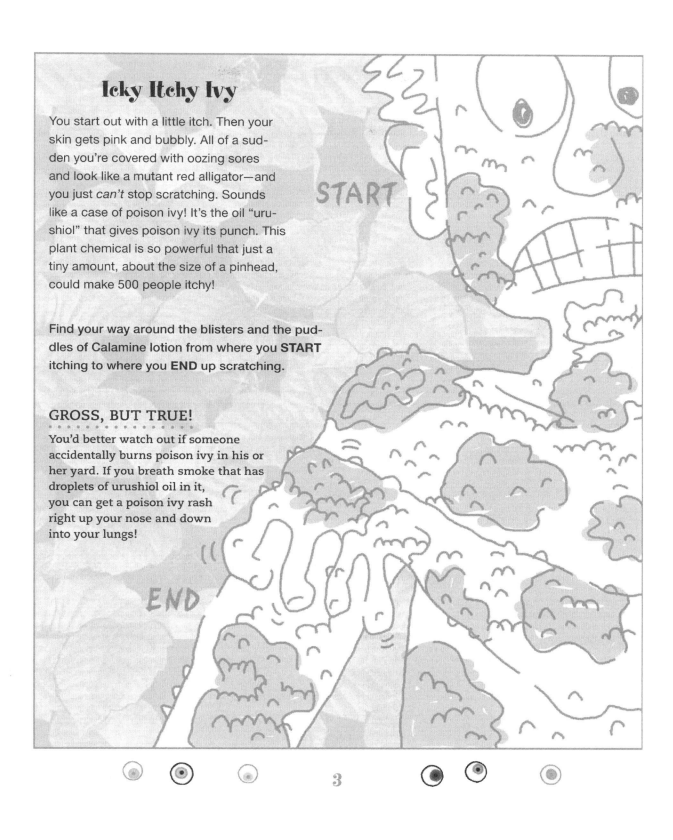

START

END

Wacky Warts

Some people hate their warts so much they chew them off! While a doctor would tell you that is a "no no," modern medicine isn't much different. Doctors burn off warts with acid, freeze them off with liquid nitrogen, or cut them off with lasers. How else can you get rid of an ugly wart? START by collecting every word along the correct path until you END up with an old-fashioned folk remedy for warts.

Abandon Ship!

When your skin peels after a bad sunburn, it's your body's way of yelling, "Get off me!" The skin cells are so badly damaged *(it isn't called a "burn" for nothing)* that your body is throwing them away. Fried skin is of no use—it can no longer protect you from infection, keep you moist, or repair itself.

Find your way from the START of this sunburn to where the fried skin ENDs on the floor!

START

END

There's a Fungus among Us

A mushroom is a kind of plant called a fungus. Believe it or not, there is one kind of fungus that loves to hang out on the skin of your feet—especially between the toes. All it needs is a good food supply (like some tasty dead skin cells) and some moisture (sweaty sneakers are great) and this foot fungus can go crazy. Pretty soon you'll have a case of itching, burning, smelly athlete's foot!

A Change of Face

Some people will do anything to get younger-looking skin. They'll let doctors blast their face with lasers to vaporize the outer layer *(it is supposed to grow back fresh and new).* Or doctors will slice down the side of their face and puuuull the loose skin tighter *(extra skin is cut off).* Maybe they will get injections of toxins right into their face to paralyze wrinkles into lying flat. Lovely!

Can you find the way from where this face STARTs to stretch to where it finally ENDs?

START

END

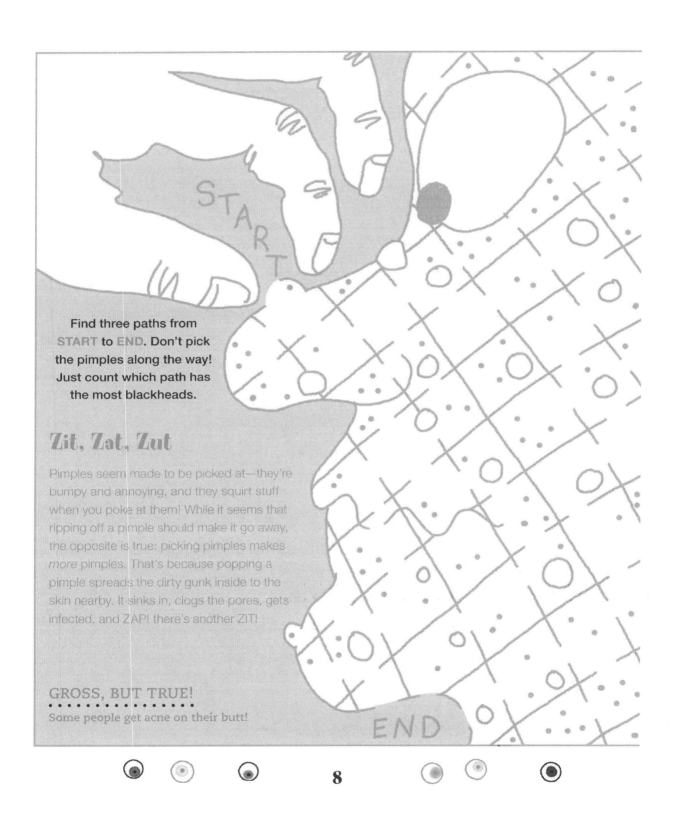

Find three paths from START to END. Don't pick the pimples along the way! Just count which path has the most blackheads.

Zit, Zat, Zut

Pimples seem made to be picked at—they're bumpy and annoying, and they squirt stuff when you poke at them! While it seems that ripping off a pimple should make it go away, the opposite is true: picking pimples makes *more* pimples. That's because popping a pimple spreads the dirty gunk inside to the skin nearby. It sinks in, clogs the pores, gets infected, and ZAP! there's another ZIT!

GROSS, BUT TRUE!
Some people get acne on their butt!

Mud Bath

How would you like to get covered in mud? Not just a little mud, like when you play soccer in a muddy field, but *totally* smeared with a thick, gooey layer of mud on your face, covering your ears, and even plastered in your hair? While your mom might send you right into a shower if you came home that gunky, some people pay a lot of money at health spas to get packed with mud. They believe the treatment is good for the skin!

Coming Through

Many people would barf at the thought of sticking a piece of metal through their skin. But that is exactly what happens when someone gets the skin of his or her ears, eyebrows, lips, or bellybutton pierced! Other people think piercing the skin is cool. In fact, the person who holds the world record for the most body piercings has almost 2,000—with more than **200** just on the face!

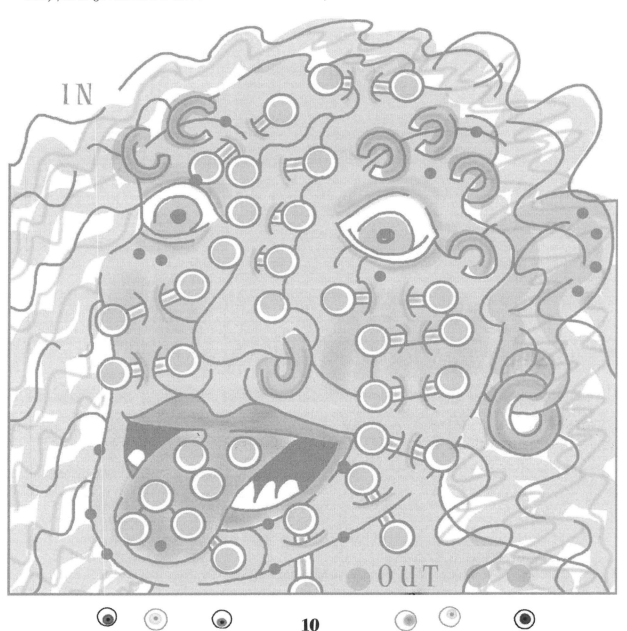

Most of the dust in your bathroom is shed skin cells! This is especially true if you really rub hard with a towel when getting dry.

Can't Stop Shedding

Crash! Bang! Clunk! What's that noise? The sound of 30,000 dead skin cells hitting the floor EVERY MINUTE! That's right—all day, all night, the top layer of your skin is falling off. By the end of the year, you will have lost more than ½ pound of skin. If you live to be 80 years old, that's about 40 pounds of skin cells! Better get out the vacuum cleaner . . .

Patches

Got a hole in your favorite jeans? Patch it! Got a hole in your skin? You can patch that, too!

If you've had a really bad burn, an accident, or surgery, you might need a new piece of skin to fix the hole. Doctors can peel a piece of healthy skin from your thigh, or even your butt, to make the patch. If that's not enough, they might use a kind of fake skin, or maybe even borrow some from a cadaver (*dead body*)! **START** stitching until you **END** up with a totally patched person.

START

END

Brain Drain

When turning a dead body into a mummy, ancient Egyptians wanted to preserve the most important parts. The lungs, liver, stomach, and intestines were removed and saved in special jars. The heart was taken out, wrapped neatly in linen, and then returned to the body. The brain? The ancient Egyptians didn't give the brain much thought. It was pulled out through the nose by a hook and thrown away!

START at the hook in the nose and **END** at out it goes!

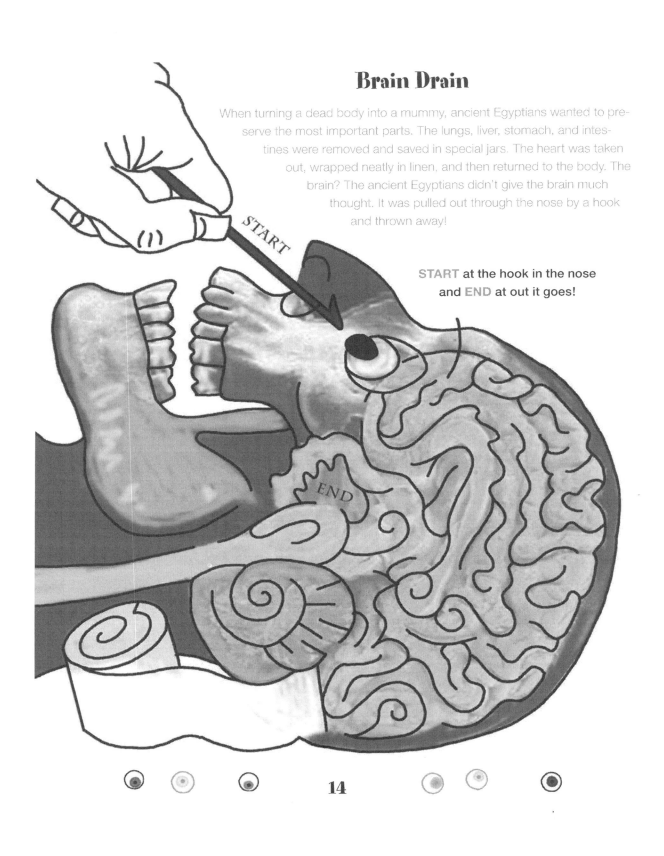

Modern Mummies

What material is used as a clear film to cover smelly food, stretched into bags to grab stinky garbage, and made into bottles to hold all sorts of slimy stuff? Plastic of course! So what better material to use when making a modern mummy! In the process called "plastination," all of the fluids and fats in a dead body are replaced with special plastics.

The end result is a mummy that is flexible, doesn't smell, and never rots.

Find the one path that leads you into every nook and cranny of this body. Don't cross over yourself!

START

Most of these modern mummies are used for research and education, but some have been featured in art exhibits!

END

Can I Have a T-shirt?

Hundreds of years ago, travelers to South America would bring home weird souvenirs—**shrunken heads!**

They had been made by native clans as trophies after a successful war against neighboring clans. Taking an enemy's head was supposed to paralyze his spirit so it couldn't continue the war. The stolen head was carefully boiled, scraped, stuffed with hot rocks and sand, and finally hung over a fire to dry. Since the skull could not be shrunk, it was removed before the process began. It was left as a gift to the snakes!

END

Are You in There?

In the eighteenth and nineteenth centuries, many people were afraid of being buried alive. Doctors might double check newly dead bodies by poking them with sharp pins, blowing horns in their ears, or stuffing spicy horseradish in their mouth. Some people made their family promise to have their head cut off or their heart removed before they were buried, just to be sure!

START at the head that's supposed to be dead—END at the friend who is shocked that it talked!

START

END

I always hated that tie!

No Vacancy

At one time, the most popular place to be buried was in a churchyard. So what happened when there were only a few churches and a LOT of bodies to be buried? Coffins would end up stacked on top of one another in the graves, and the churchyards kept getting higher and higher. Some churches had to build sturdy stone walls around their yards to keep body parts from falling out into the street! **You'd better START now if you want to END up in this cemetery.**

Z-Z-Z-Zombies

AAARGH!! They look like sleepwalkers—shuffling slowly, arms outstretched, no expression on their faces. The only difference is they are coming to get YOU! And once they do, they will either eat your brains, or turn you into a zombie just like they are. Since zombies are already dead, how do you stop them?

START by renting a zombie movie. Watch it all the way to the **END**!

Crash Test Bodies?

Companies that make cars need to know how much force it takes to break an arm or squash a kneecap. That's because they have to build cars safe enough to keep that from happening in an accident. However, not many people would volunteer to test what happens in a car crash, and plastic crash test robots need to act like real bodies. So how do car makers figure out how real bodies act in a crash? They have helpful dead bodies test the cars out first!

Tests START with new cars and END up with wrecked ones.

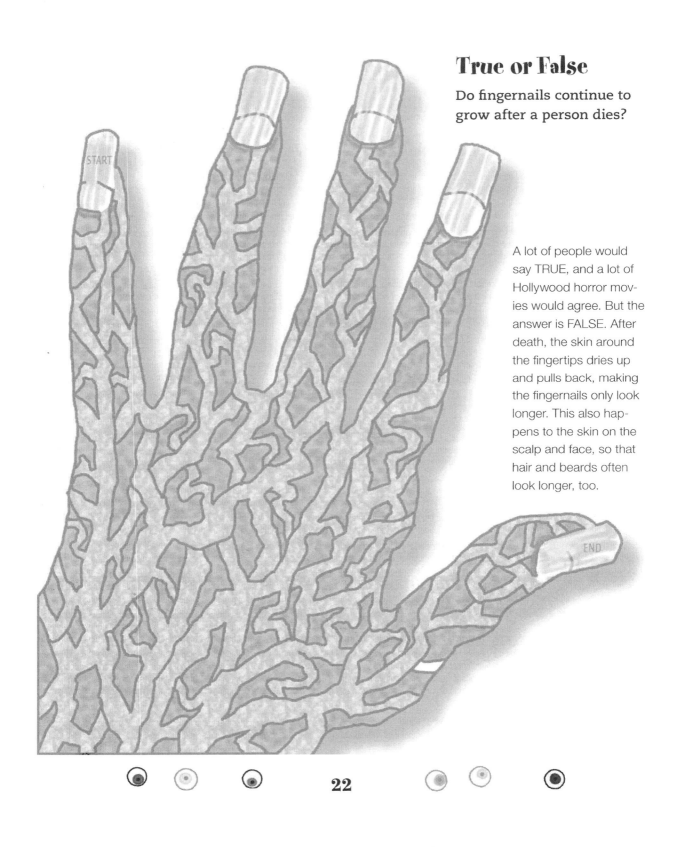

True or False

Do fingernails continue to grow after a person dies?

A lot of people would say TRUE, and a lot of Hollywood horror movies would agree. But the answer is FALSE. After death, the skin around the fingertips dries up and pulls back, making the fingernails only look longer. This also happens to the skin on the scalp and face, so that hair and beards often look longer, too.

START

END

Lend a Hand

Modern surgeons know a lot about how the human body works, but that wasn't always true. Hundreds of years ago it was illegal to cut up a human body to study it. Some medical students had to sneak the bodies they needed . . . by robbing graves! A body was usually safe if the person died in the summer because it would rot too fast for a surgeon to have time to dig it up. But if someone died in the cold weather, he or she would need a locked iron casket or a watchman with a rifle to protect their remains!

See if you can make a single path through the graveyard to collect all the parts this sneaky student needs to make an entire person. Your path cannot cross over itself.

Dead Men DO Tell Tales!

A lot of TV shows feature investigators carefully checking clues at a crime scene. The biggest clue is often a dead body. But what can it tell? For one thing, scientists know what types of bugs they will find on a body that has been left outdoors. They know exactly how long it takes each kind of bug to reproduce and grow. The size and number of bugs can be used as a gross, but accurate, clock to tell how long a body has been dead!

If the cop **START**s looking at these bugs, he might **END** up knowing when the murder happened.

24

S.S.S. *(Shed Snake Skin)*

Have you ever found a long, crumpled strip of what looks like deflated bubble wrap in your yard? You were probably looking at a snake's skin! Unlike people, who shed lots of little skin cells every day, a snake peels off a whole layer of dead scales all at once. If you look closely at the shed skin, you will even see the transparent scales that once covered the snake's eyeballs!

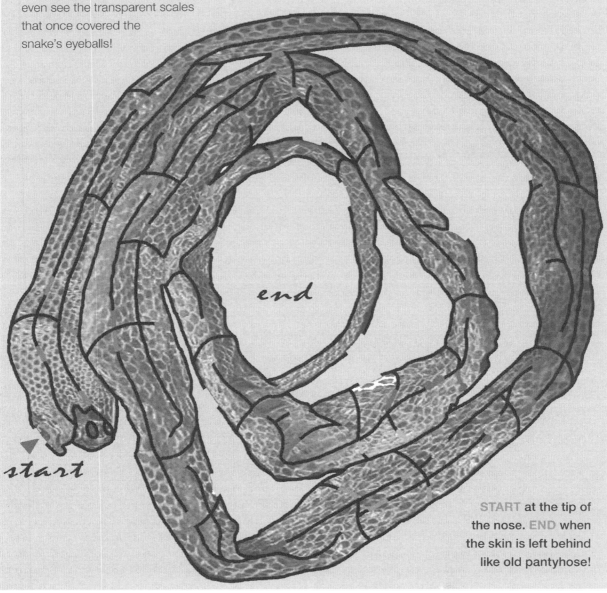

end

start

START at the tip of the nose. END when the skin is left behind like old pantyhose!

H.D.C. *(Hot Dog Casings)*

If you eat "natural casing" franks, your lunch will contain an unexpected ingredient—intestines! The clear, plastic-looking skin on the outside of a natural hot dog actually comes from the inside of a sheep! You'll be happy to know that before you ever bite your hot dog, the casing has had the poop, fat, and whiskers *(blood vessels)* removed. **START** eating!

T.H. *(Tomato Hornworms)*

If you grow tomatoes in your yard, you have probably seen HUGE, green caterpillars on the plants. This is the tomato hornworm, and it can munch a tomato vine right down to the skeleton. However, the little Cotesia wasp just loves the T.H. Why? The wasp lays its eggs inside the hornworm. As the eggs hatch, the larvae eat the caterpillar from the inside out—while the hornworm is still alive! Eventually the little wasps chew through the hornworm's skin and spin tiny cocoons all down its back.

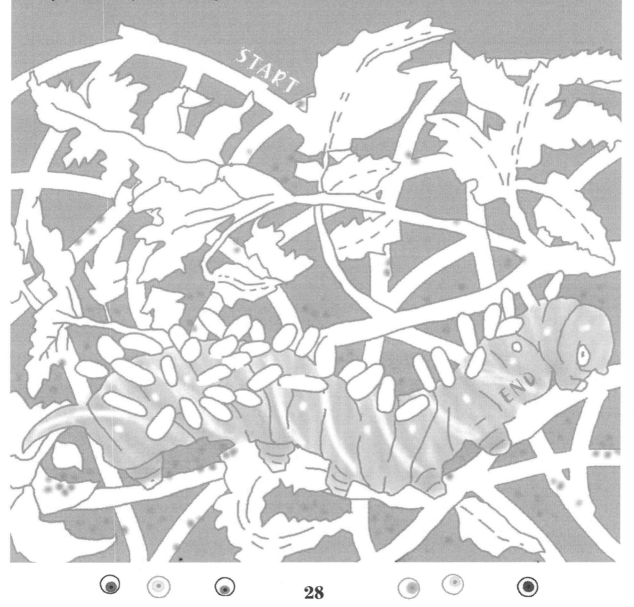

B.B. *(Beach Blobs)*

Have you ever gone walking on the beach after a storm and found hundreds of jelly-like blobs? Don't step on them with your bare feet, because you might get a sting—those harmless looking blobs are moon jellyfish. Even if they are dead, their harpoon-like stinging cells still work!

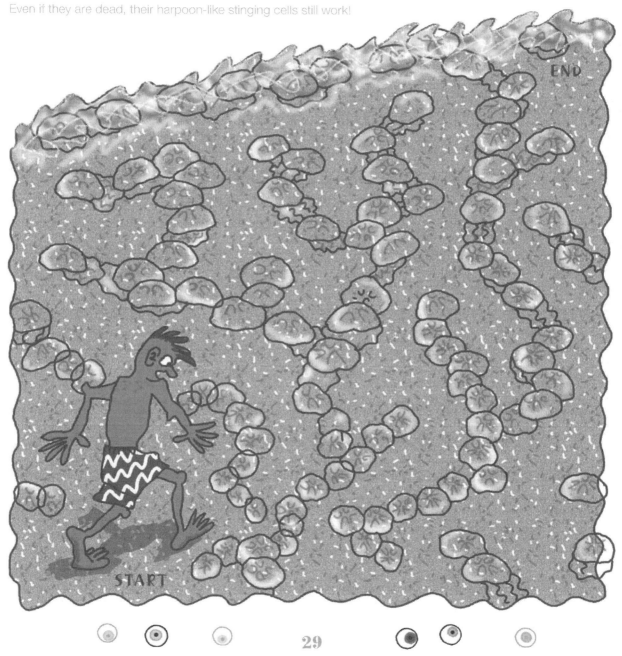

Y.D.V. *(Yellow Dog Vomit)*

You're walking through the park one warm summer day, and there in the bark mulch is a puddle of what looks like bright yellow dog vomit. This lovely lawn decoration is called a "slime mold." Believe it or not, that yellow blob is actually one giant cell, kind of like a mutant, moving egg yolk. When it is time for the slime mold to reproduce, it changes—then it will look like crusty pancake, with blood-like red "sauce" on top!

Can you stand to slither through this slime mold from **START** to **END**?

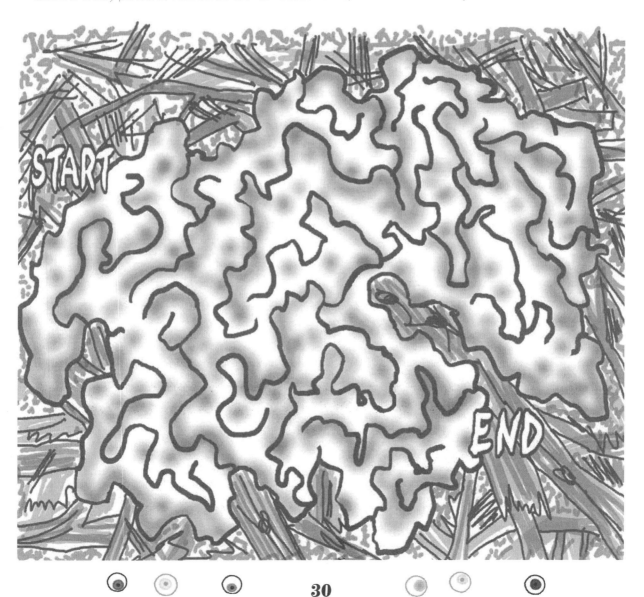

E.T. *(Exploding Toads)*

If you walked through a park in Hamburg, Germany, in spring of 2005, you might have seen slimy green and red puddles on the sidewalk. Hmmm . . . does that look familiar? Could it be . . . a toad? An exploded toad? What's going on!? No one could figure out why more than 1,000 toads mysteriously swelled up and then burst in a shower of toad guts. One theory is that crows pecked out the toads' livers!

Can you START through this puddle and END up not walking on any toad guts?

D.G. *(Dugout Glop)*

Chew and spit, and chew and spit . . . why do baseball players chew and spit? Well, baseball fields are naturally dusty places, so chewing tobacco, gum, or sunflower seeds helps to keep the players' mouths moist. Plus players may not want to swallow all the water they swill to wash away the dust. But if you need to spit a zillion times, where you gonna do it? On the dugout floor!

Which player spits the most? Follow the three paths to find out.
Add the number on each player's uniform to the number on his spit puddle.
The highest total number wins!

F.F.B.
(Forest Furballs)

Walking through the woods, you might find an odd looking furball on the ground. Look closer and you might see a bone poking out, perhaps even a tiny foot or a tail. What is this thing? It's an owl pellet! Owls don't chew their food like you do. They swallow mice and other small rodents whole. Their stomach squishes out the edible parts, and the parts they can't digest (fur and bones) get pressed into a pellet. Before the owl can eat again, it has to make room in its gut. How? It barfs up the pellet!

What STARTs out as a whole mouse ENDs up as a pile of mouse bones!

END

START

P.W.N. *(Paper Wasp Nest)*

Ever see something that looks like a gray Christmas ornament hanging from the edge of a house? Look more closely and you'll see little paper cells all joined together, and white, wiggling heads poking out. Eeeew, what is that? You've just found a paper wasp nest! The wasps mix chewed-up plant fibers with spit to make their papery home. A single egg is laid in each cell and then hatches into a legless grub. Be careful—the worker wasps who feed chewed-up caterpillars to the grubs also protect the nest.

START backing away from the nest before
a wasp **END**s up stinging you!

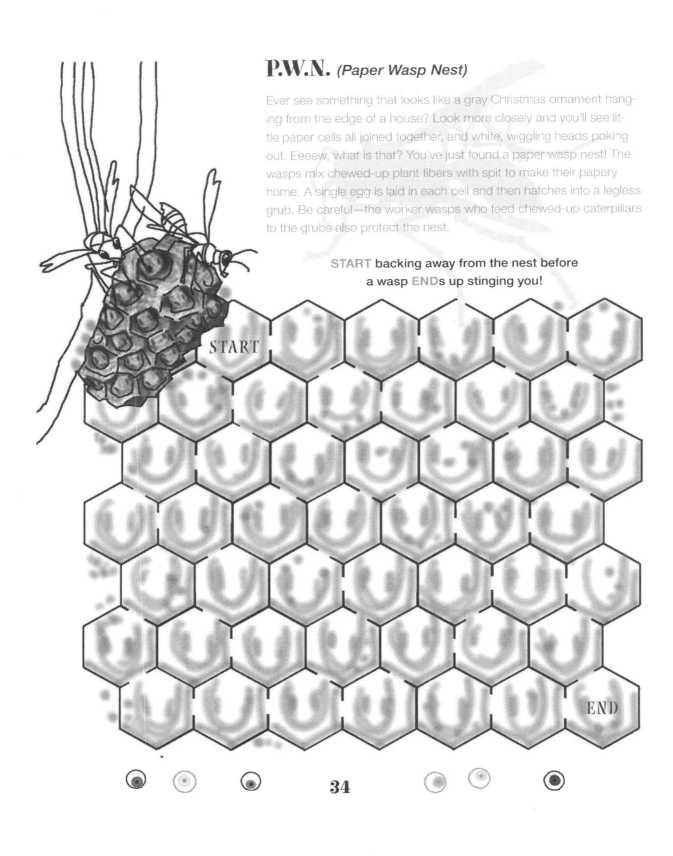

START

END

F.W.B. *(Floating White Blobs)*

Have you ever found a white, rubbery blob floating in the swimming pool? Watch out—it's a poop packet from a baby bird! Every time an adult bird stuffs a worm in a baby's beak, poop comes out the other end. To clean the nest, a parent bird picks up the poop and carries it away. Actually, for the first few days after the baby birds have hatched, the parents simply swallow the packets. The poop inside is full of barely digested food, and the adult birds don't want to waste it!

START at the baby bird's butt, and see where the poop packet ENDs up.

U.D.C. *(Under Desk Crunchies)*

Run your fingers under the edge of any school table—what is all that gunk under there? The bulk of it *(crunchy and sharp)* is boogers. Next up is probably gum *(smooth, hard wads)*. If you find something kind of wet and mushy, it's probably a spitball. Find something slimy? Who knows what that might be, except *really* gross!

Start feeling around until you find out which gross goodie each kid left under the table!

   36

Chapter 4

Getting Dirty

Scraping Slime

Hagfish release HUGE amounts of thick slime that suffocates attackers who get too close. How does it get rid of extra slime once the attack is over? The hagfish twists its flexible body into a knot. Then it passes the knot all the way from head to tail, scraping off the extra goop as it goes!

Can you guess the hagfish's nickname? Collect the letters as you follow the maze.

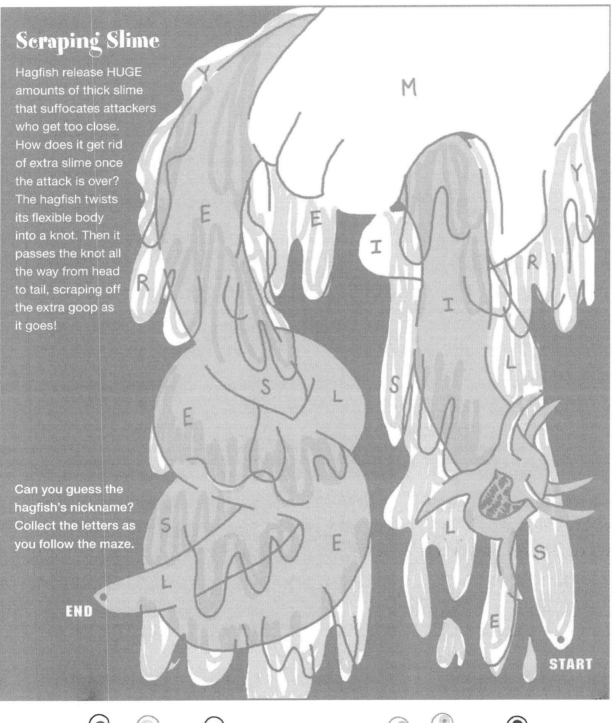

END

START

SPLAT!

How would you like a gooshy, rotten tomato smeared down your back, splattered in your ear, or even squished right in your face? If you are in Buñol, Spain, the last Wednesday of August, you are sure to get totally covered in tomato gunk. Every year the whole town, and thousands of visitors, join in the Tomatina—a huge tomato fight! START throwing tomatoes. Can you find two paths to SPLAT the target?

GROSS, BUT TRUE!

By the end of the festival, the streets of Buñol run red with tomato juice! The town has to be cleaned with fire hoses.

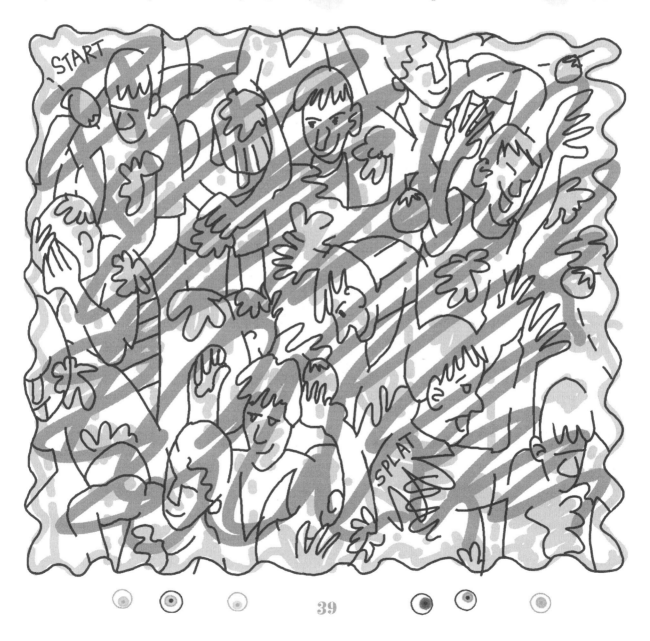

Hard Water

It's hard to know whether the ancient Greeks were getting clean or dirty when they took a bath. First they would rub themselves all over with sand and olive oil. Sometimes they would add clay and even ashes to the mix. Then they would take a special metal tool called a "strigil" and scrape off all the gritty greasy stuff they had just slathered on. Apparently they hoped to scrape off the dirt, too!

START scraping and see if you END up clean!

START

HEY!

END

Soapy Stew

When early American settlers wanted soap, they couldn't go to the corner store and buy some. They had to start by slaughtering a pig or cow! Then, hunks of animal fat would be put in a big kettle of water and boiled until the fat melted. This process got rid of all the blood, meat, and other animal tissues. After the fat cooled and floated to the top of the kettle, it was mixed with lye (made from ashes) to make a very strong soap. If there was no fresh fat to use, creative settlers would use the fat left over from cooking their dinner!

START boiling 'til you **END** up with some nice, clean fat!

Clean Cats

If you had no washcloth or bar of soap, how might you get clean? Well, if you were as flexible as a cat and had a nice raspy tongue, you could lick yourself all over! There are two problems with this. One is that the spikes on a cat's tongue all point to the back of his mouth, so any hair stuck on the tongue gets swallowed, not spit out. After a while all this extra hair mixes with mucus *(the same body fluid that makes snot)* and forms a hairball. Gack! The other problem is that if you lick yourself all over, you end up covered with spit!

END

START

START cleaning this cat's paw, and **END** at the tip of his tail.

Next!

Before homes had electricity, it was not easy to take a bath. Water had to be pumped by hand, carried into the house, and heated on the stove. After all that effort, you didn't throw the bathwater out after just one person had used it. The daddy took his bath first, then all the way on down the line to the youngest. Some new hot water might have been added from time to time, but basically everyone shared the same tub of suds!

START at dad and wash your way to the **END** of the line.
Don't skip anyone!

START

END

Scoop the Poop!

Everyone knows that dogs gotta go—too bad many dogs
go where people also like to run and walk! Can you find
the path that helps the soccer player reach the **END** of
the game while dodging the doo-doo? Even better, find a
second path that **END**s up scooping four of the six plops.
Make sure the two paths do *NOT* cross over each other.

soccer
player
start

pooper
scooper
start

END

Can't Blink, Gotta Slurp!

START

END

Little green geckos have very large eyes, but they don't have any eyelids! When a gecko's eye gets dusty or covered with gunk, how does it get clean? Simple—the gecko uses its very long tongue to lick its eye clean! Can you help these five geckos clean up?

Lid Down!

Boys, does your mom nag you to close the toilet lid when you're done? Well, it's not only so the next person won't fall in. It's because research has shown that when you flush a toilet with the lid up, all kinds of microscopic stuff *(especially pee)* goes airborne. It covers the toilet, the floor, the walls, and can even spray the ceiling! Oh, and you'd better store your toothbrush far away from the toilet, or who knows what you'll be brushing with.

Can you find both paths to the toothbrush?

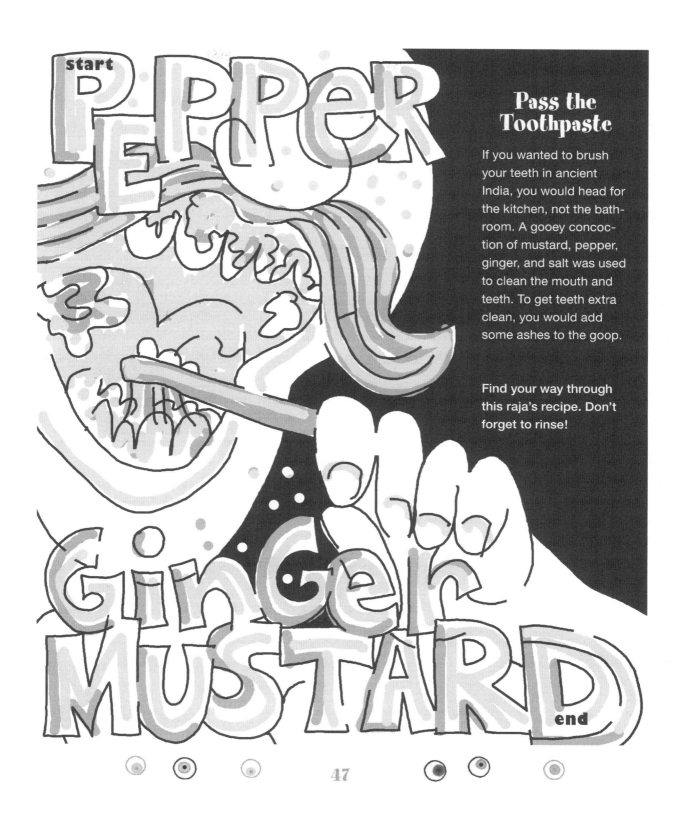

Pass the Toothpaste

If you wanted to brush your teeth in ancient India, you would head for the kitchen, not the bathroom. A gooey concoction of mustard, pepper, ginger, and salt was used to clean the mouth and teeth. To get teeth extra clean, you would add some ashes to the goop.

Find your way through this raja's recipe. Don't forget to rinse!

Hair and Gone

Some people just don't want hair in certain places. To clean it off they will shave, pluck, and even use chemicals that dissolve hair completely. Here's one more method: hot wax is spread on top of the hair and skin. When it cools, the hair is firmly stuck to the wax. Then, when the wax is yanked away from the skin, it will rip all the hair out, including the roots. Ouch!

Lose Your Lunch

What do you do if you're a mommy pelican and have to carry food to several hungry chicks? Since a pelican doesn't have hands or pockets, the easiest way to carry food is to swallow it. Back at the nest, momma bird upchucks the almost digested fish for the chicks to eat. As the chicks get bigger and hungrier, they will stick their heads into momma's beak to get the goodies. A really hungry chick will reach right down her throat!

START slurping till you reach the **END** of this moist and mushy meal!

START

END

Space Toilet

On Earth, gravity makes poop plop into the toilet. But in outer space there is no gravity! That's why NASA developed a high-tech toilet that uses a vacuum to suck poop down into a special container. There are even straps to hold the astronaut in place while he or she "goes." FYI: For liquid waste, each person has his or her own personal suction funnel.

Oops, smelly "asteroids" are floating all over the inside of the space shuttle. Someone accidentally turned the suction off! How fast can you help the astronaut reach the switch to turn it back on?

Tooting Termites

Termites are small, ant-like insects. Individually, each termite isn't very special. But put two or three million of them together, and they are world-class producers. Of what? Farts! These insects are always working and always hungry. They eat huge amounts of wood and woody plants. This high-fiber diet produces a lot of termite farts. In fact, it has been estimated that in one year, termites add 150 million tons of methane (fart) gas into the atmosphere!

Find your way through the termite fumes from **START** to **END**.

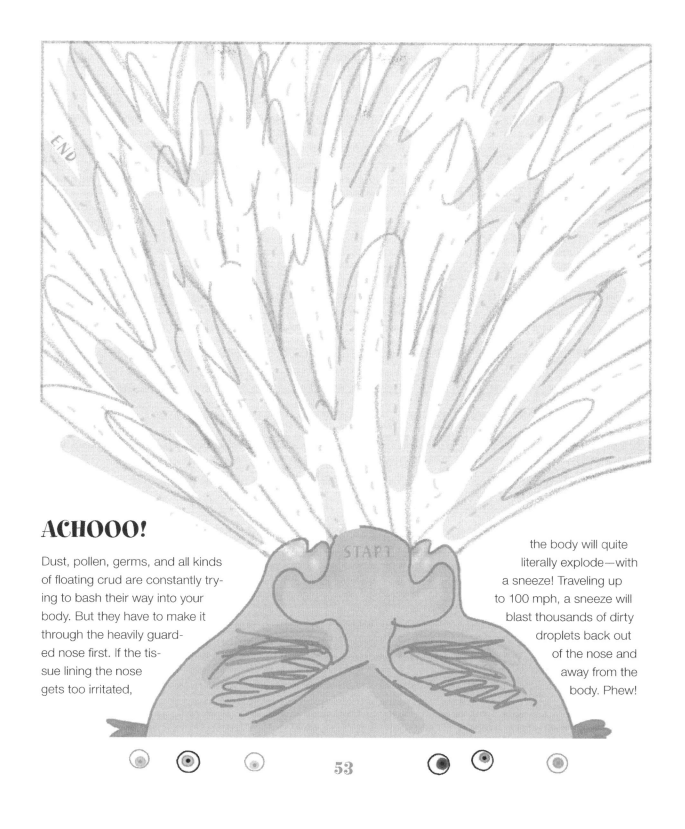

ACHOOO!

Dust, pollen, germs, and all kinds of floating crud are constantly trying to bash their way into your body. But they have to make it through the heavily guarded nose first. If the tissue lining the nose gets too irritated, the body will quite literally explode—with a sneeze! Traveling up to 100 mph, a sneeze will blast thousands of dirty droplets back out of the nose and away from the body. Phew!

Stand Back

Sea cucumbers look harmless. They slowly ooze along the ocean floor, using sticky tentacles to snarf up any edible particles *(like poop)*. But if a hungry fish tries to bite a cucumber, watch out. This squishy sea creature defends itself by vomiting out its entire digestive system, and sometimes even its breathing tubes! While the predator is distracted by this blast of internal organs, the sea cucumber escapes.

START
Follow the guts over and under.

END

I hate it when he does that!

Twice as Good

The food that rabbits eat isn't very nutritious. To get the most from a meal, rabbits must digest their food twice. How do they do this? They eat their poops! After eating a meal, rabbits poop out soft, green, squishy pellets. Rabbits eat this poop right away, while it is fresh and warm. Later they poop again, except these pellets are hard, brown, and dry. The bunnies leave those poops alone. All done!

Find your way from **START** to **END**. Your path must go through the bunny!

Zip It Up

Mountains and forests are beautiful places to camp. But if enough people travel through a scenic spot and leave their poop behind, suddenly the scenery isn't so nice anymore! That's why a lot of national parks have rules that any poop made while you're in the park must be carried home with you, not left for others to "enjoy." Plastic bags that zip closed work great for carrying caca. That's convenient, because campers can carry out the poop in the same bags they used to carry in the food!

Put the poop IN the bag and carry it OUT.

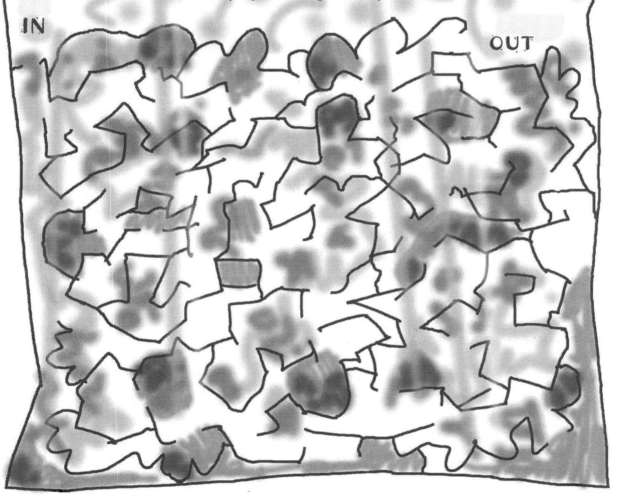

Knock, Knock

The correct path **START**s on the top row and **END**s on the bottom row, spelling out a gross joke on the way.

START

Knock,	knock.	Who's	there?	Fajita.
knock.	Fajita.	there?	who?	Fajita,
who?	Fajita,	nother	Fajita	nother
Fajita	nother	bite,	I'm	going
nother	bite,	I'm	throw	to
bite,	I'm		up!	throw

Spew for Science

Scientists in England were happy to discover a pile of fossilized vomit estimated to be 160 million years old! Turns out that ichthyosaurs *(ancient marine reptiles)* ate a lot of shellfish that looked like squids. The difference was that these prehistoric squids had a hard, pointy shell that ichthyosaurs couldn't digest. Since the shells would rip up the digestive tract on the way out the back end, icthyosaurs simply threw up the shells!

Garbage In, Fertilizer Out

What is one of the best ways to turn a pile of vegetable scraps into fertilizer for your garden? Run it through the digestive system of a worm! A bin full of hundreds of wriggling red worms can quickly convert carrot peels and apple cores to nutrient-rich worm poop *(called casings)*. In fact, the liquid that seeps out of the bottom of a worm farm is good for the garden, too. It's called "worm tea"!

START

END

Have you ever laughed so hard that whatever you were eating came out your nose? Some people think this is such a great trick that they practice doing it on purpose! In fact, a man who can shoot a noodle 7½ inches out of his nose holds the world record. He can even get the other end of the strand to come out of the other nostril! For this maze it is okay to go over and under lines.

Terrible Teeth

Many people believe President George Washington's false teeth were made of wood. Actually, his dentures were made of ivory from a hippopotamus! Worse yet, shortly before his inauguration ceremony, George had his dentures overhauled. The dentist replaced eight of the hippo teeth with teeth from a fresh cadaver *(dead body)*. George is STARTing to think that his teeth will be the END of him!

62

Jeepers, Creepers, Where'd You Get Those Peepers?

What happens if, because of an accident or illness, you lose an eye? Today, there are lightweight plastic replacements that can be made to exactly match your remaining eye. These modern eyes are even designed to move in a natural way. But back in the 1800s, "glass eyes" were really made of glass! Eye doctors would stock a variety of sizes and colors. To find the best fit, you would have to go to the doctor's office and try on the eyes. The office usually held hundreds of eyes, in cabinets, boxes, and drawers!

START at the top row, and **END** when you have found the perfect fit.

Did You Lose This?

Some creatures don't need help with body part replacements. They grow their own! A fast-moving lizard can break off its tail if grabbed by a predator. Within a few months it will grow back almost as good as new, just slightly shorter, a different color, and with cartilage instead of bone! A starfish can regrow a new arm (or two), and the sea cucumber can regrow a whole new digestive system!

Can you find the one lizard that did not lose its tail?

I've Been Scalped!

If a balding man doesn't like his looks, doctors can help replace the hair that's been lost. Actually, they just move it around a little bit. Using new techniques, doctors "harvest" small bundles of hair from one area, and transplant them into a bald area. Hundreds of tiny cuts are used to carefully place the bundles so they look natural. But one type of surgery popular in the 1980s did not look natural. "Scalp flap" surgery was just as gross as it sounds. Incisions were made in the back of the head, and a flap of skin with the hair growing in it would be rotated to a bald part of the head and stitched in place.

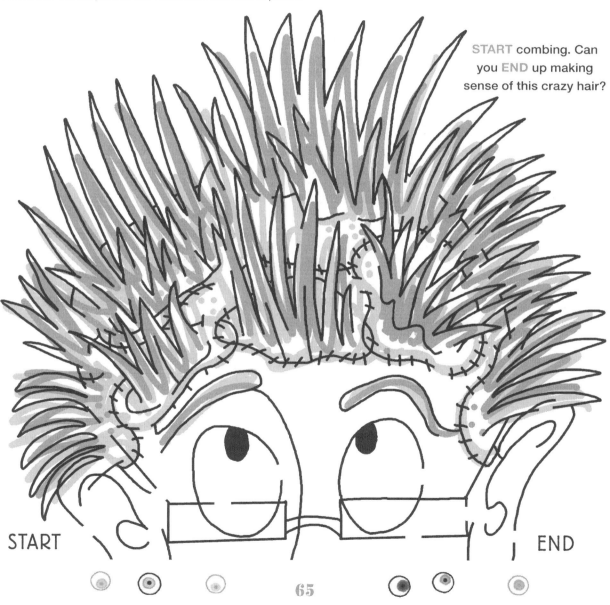

START combing. Can you END up making sense of this crazy hair?

START

END

Fill in the Face

Bad accidents, or even bad acne, can leave scars that look like potholes in your skin. A replacement of some sort is needed to fill the hole and make the damaged skin more smooth and healthy looking. A natural protein would work best, but where can that be found? Some doctors use a protein called collagen that is removed from cadavers *(dead people).* While the idea of cadaver skin inside their face bothers some patients, others think it's OK. They may even choose to use it for cosmetic reasons, like making thin lips look plumper!

START filling in the holes. How does this face look at the END?

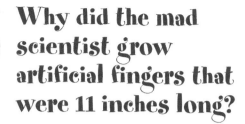

Why did the mad scientist grow artificial fingers that were 11 inches long?

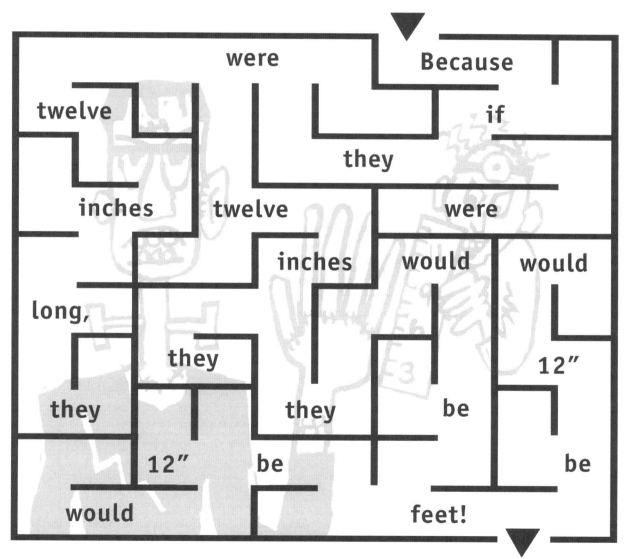

were

Because

twelve

if

they

inches   twelve   were

inches   would   would

long,

they

they   they   be

12"   be   feet!   be

would

Lost and Found

Modern replacement limbs are pretty amazing. With a replacement leg, an average person can walk, and an athlete can run a marathon! But there's one type of arm or leg that is not such a good replacement. The so-called phantom, or ghost, limb. This is when someone who has lost an arm or leg still feels like the lost limb is attached to his or her body. They may think it's moving, or they may feel pain in it. Some people even get the sensation that they have an extra arm or leg!

Got Blood?

Be happy that you don't live in the year 1873. At that time blood transfusions were still pretty new, and doctors didn't quite have the hang of them yet. If you had a bad accident and needed extra blood, you might have ended up with a transfusion of milk instead! By 1884, so many people had had bad reactions to milk transfusions (duh!) that doctors started using salt water instead. It wasn't until 1907 that transfusions of blood started to become safe and routine.

START the transfusion. See what **ENDs** up in the patient!

How to Fix a Broken Heart

The heart is a complicated organ, full of chambers and valves and muscles pumping blood under tremendous pressure. You don't just stroll down to the corner store to pick up spare parts—or do you? Doctors have learned how to replace a bad valve in a human heart by using valves from the heart of a pig. These valves are most often collected when pigs are processed into pork products like the ones you eat for dinner!

START flowing through this heart. Can you find the pig valve before you reach the **END**?

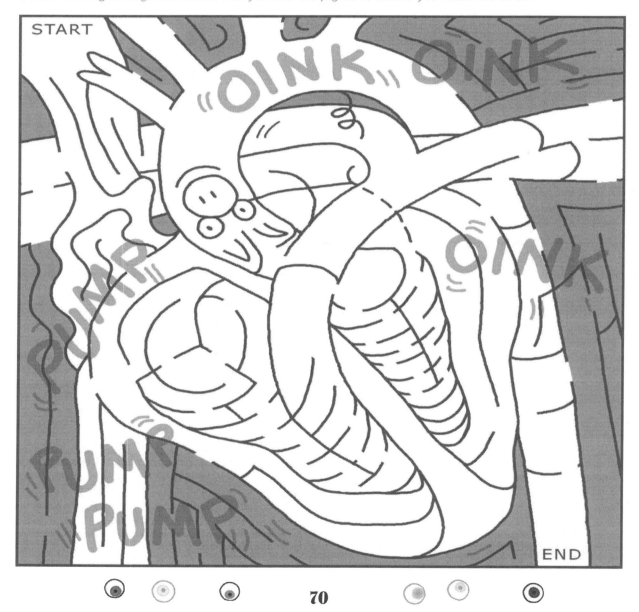

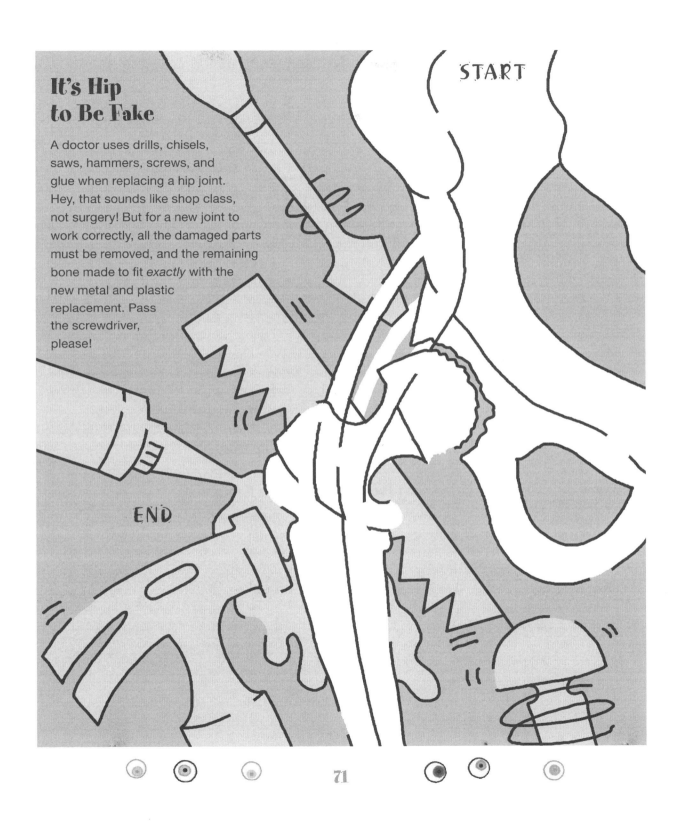

It's Hip to Be Fake

A doctor uses drills, chisels, saws, hammers, screws, and glue when replacing a hip joint. Hey, that sounds like shop class, not surgery! But for a new joint to work correctly, all the damaged parts must be removed, and the remaining bone made to fit *exactly* with the new metal and plastic replacement. Pass the screwdriver, please!

I See You

There is a clear lens inside of your eye that focuses light and makes it possible for you to see. As a person ages, this lens can get cloudy and make vision lousy. But there is a way to replace the old, cloudy lens with a new, crystal clear one. That's great! However, the surgery involves cutting into the eye to remove the old lens. That's gross!

GROSS, BUT TRUE!

As far back as Roman times, people tried to remove cataracts. Except back then they used a thin needle, or even a thin stick, to push the cloudy lens out of the way.

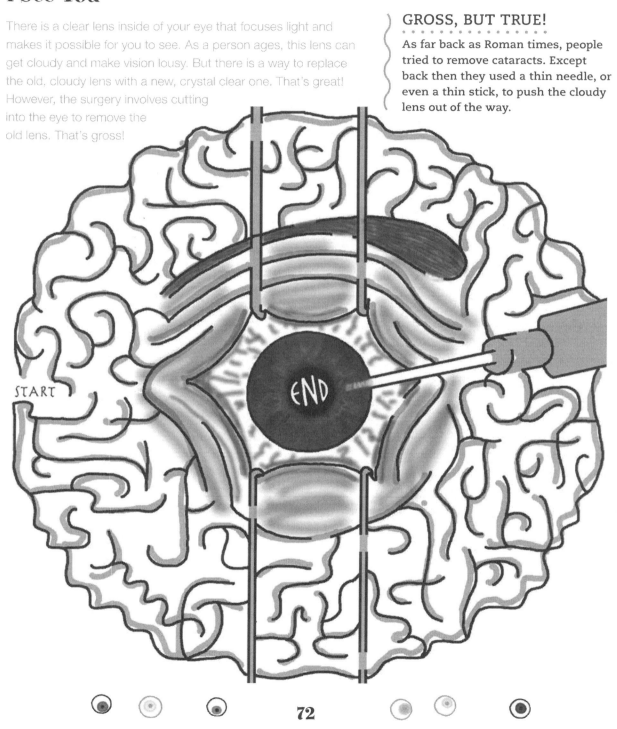

START

END

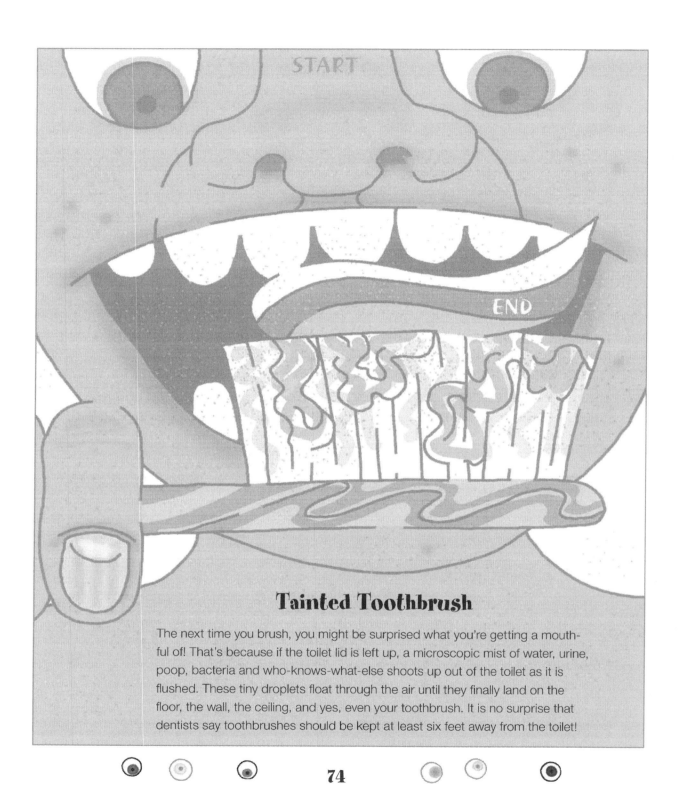

START

END

Tainted Toothbrush

The next time you brush, you might be surprised what you're getting a mouth-ful of! That's because if the toilet lid is left up, a microscopic mist of water, urine, poop, bacteria and who-knows-what-else shoots up out of the toilet as it is flushed. These tiny droplets float through the air until they finally land on the floor, the wall, the ceiling, and yes, even your toothbrush. It is no surprise that dentists say toothbrushes should be kept at least six feet away from the toilet!

Bzzzzz, SLAP!

Mosquito bites are such a part of a summer's evening that most people don't even think about them. But what's really going on when that miniature menace bites you? First, it's only the female mosquitoes that bite. That long needle-like appendage she bites with is actually her mouth! Mrs. Mosquito stabs your skin, then squirts in a dose of saliva. Her special spit has chemicals that stop your blood from clotting *(getting thick and lumpy).* That makes blood much easier to slurp!

This mosquito is STARTing to feed. When will she END?

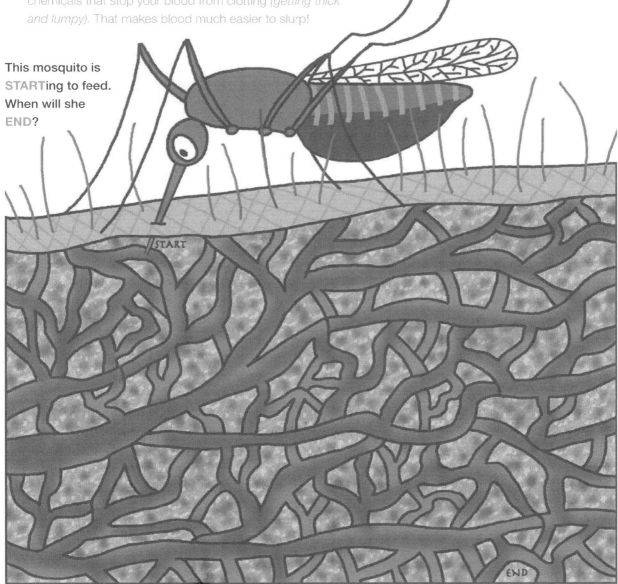

START

END

Feast for a Flea

There are some facts about fleas that are cool. For instance, when an average-size flea jumps a foot off the ground to land on a passing dog, it is the same as if an average-size man jumped more than 800 feet! Then there are some facts about fleas that are just gross, like the fact that fleas feed on blood. The half-digested blood they poop out is called "flea dirt," and it's the food that baby fleas love to eat!

When the fleas START biting, the dog ENDs up scratching!

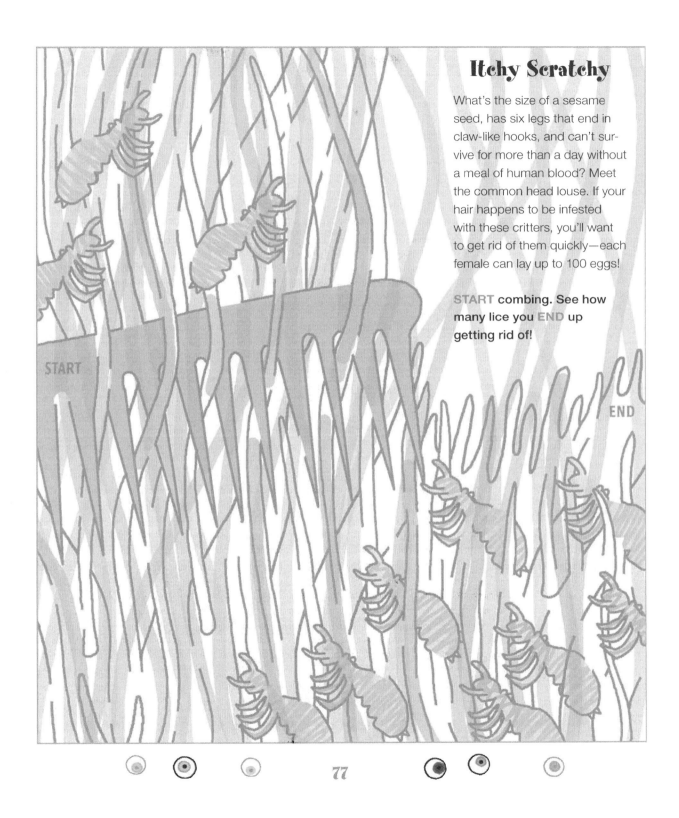

Itchy Scratchy

What's the size of a sesame seed, has six legs that end in claw-like hooks, and can't survive for more than a day without a meal of human blood? Meet the common head louse. If your hair happens to be infested with these critters, you'll want to get rid of them quickly—each female can lay up to 100 eggs!

START combing. See how many lice you **END** up getting rid of!

START

END

Gotta Run

All of a sudden you get an urgent feeling and have to run for the bathroom. You've got diarrhea! It's amazing that microscopic bacteria can cause such a dramatic explosion of poop. Our guts are actually full of helpful bacteria, but sometimes a strange germ gets in there and throws the system into a panic. Then the large intestine stops absorbing as much water as it normally does, so liquidy poop rushes through, and out, at a great rate of speed. Oops, gotta run again!

Find the path to the toilet that has the most TP—you'll need it!

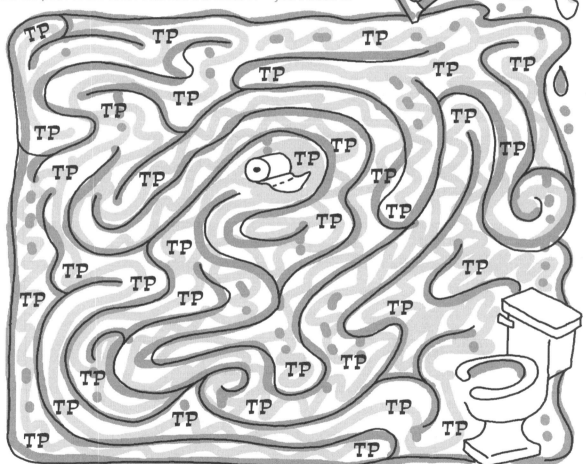

GROSS, BUT TRUE!

Many travelers unknowingly eat or drink strange bacteria and end up coming home with diarrhea as an unhappy souvenir. Bacteria can even be picked up from ice cubes!

   78

Allergy Attack

To most people, the tiny flakes of dried skin that fall off a cat aren't a problem. But cat "dander" (and cat saliva, too) can turn other people into itchy, sneezy, wheezy, nose-blowing messes. Some people also get itchy rashes, hives (lumps) on their skin, plugged-up ears, and red, watery eyes. Cat dander must be pretty powerful stuff. It can cause all these symptoms even though most of the stuff that falls off a cat is smaller than dust!

When the cat dander STARTs to fly, this man's nose ENDs up running!

79

ACHOO!

Think you're allergic to dust? Actually, the truth is a whole lot smaller. Living in your carpets, in your furniture, and even inside your pillows and mattress are incredibly tiny bugs called dust mites. These spider-like critters are so small, they can't be seen without a microscope. But just because they are tiny doesn't mean they aren't busy. All day and night they chow down on their favorite food—dead skin cells. All this munching results in a lot of pooping, and it is actually the POOP of the dust mite that makes you sneeze!

GROSS, BUT TRUE!

Have you had the same pillow on your bed for several years? Almost ten percent of the pillow's weight is made up of dead mites and their poop!

If you **START** to sneeze, it might be because of what comes out of the **END** of a dust mite!

START

END

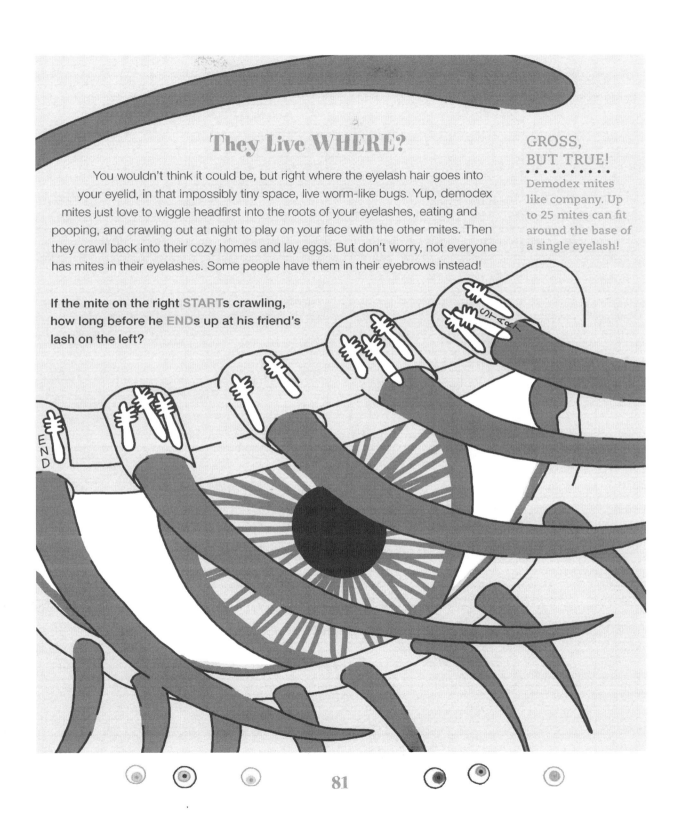

They Live WHERE?

You wouldn't think it could be, but right where the eyelash hair goes into your eyelid, in that impossibly tiny space, live worm-like bugs. Yup, demodex mites just love to wiggle headfirst into the roots of your eyelashes, eating and pooping, and crawling out at night to play on your face with the other mites. Then they crawl back into their cozy homes and lay eggs. But don't worry, not everyone has mites in their eyelashes. Some people have them in their eyebrows instead!

If the mite on the right STARTs crawling, how long before he ENDs up at his friend's lash on the left?

GROSS, BUT TRUE!
• • • • • • • • • •
Demodex mites like company. Up to 25 mites can fit around the base of a single eyelash!

END

I Vant Your Body Fluids

For such a tiny pest, a vampire mite is a big pain in the hive. The mite is only the size of a pinhead, and all it wants to do is attack honeybees. It wiggles between the tough plates that cover the bee's abdomen. Once there, it drills through the skin and sucks up all the body fluids. Then it climbs into the honeycomb where new bees are growing, and sucks the juices out of them, too!

START at the mite. **END** at the juicy bee.

Numerous Nematodes

Dog got worms? Nematodes. Carrots grow all weird and gnarly? Nematodes. Infected with hookworm, roundworm, or whipworm? Nematode, nematode, nematode. In fact, there are more than 20,000 different kinds of these worm-like critters. Many are super tiny—less than 1/100 inch. Super tiny, yes, but they can be super destructive, too. It is estimated that about 3 *billion* people on the planet are infected with nematodes. How is that possible? Well, some nematodes can lay more than 100,000 eggs in one day. Yikes!

GROSS, BUT TRUE!

While most nematodes are only fractions of an inch long, one variety grows to over 20 feet. Where can it be found? In the stomach of a sperm whale!

END

START

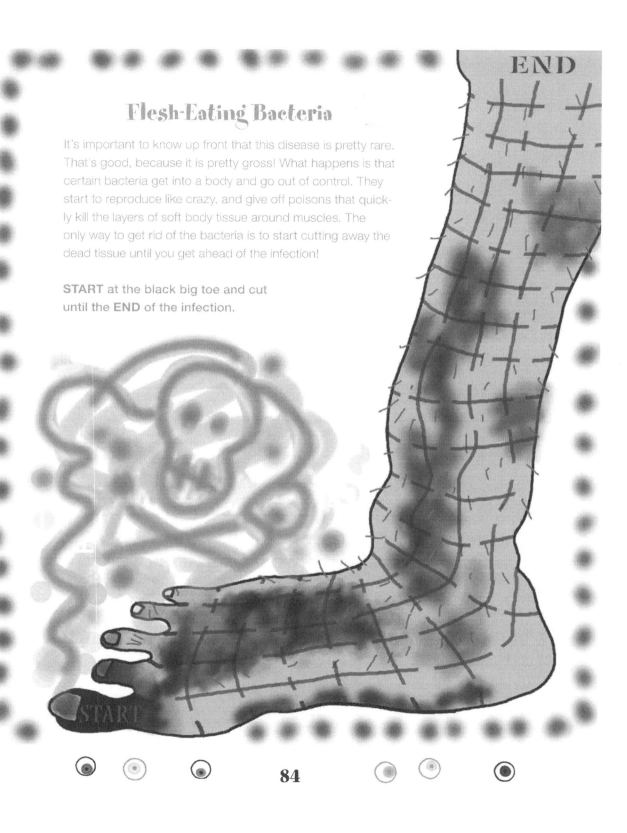

Flesh-Eating Bacteria

It's important to know up front that this disease is pretty rare. That's good, because it is pretty gross! What happens is that certain bacteria get into a body and go out of control. They start to reproduce like crazy, and give off poisons that quickly kill the layers of soft body tissue around muscles. The only way to get rid of the bacteria is to start cutting away the dead tissue until you get ahead of the infection!

START at the black big toe and cut until the **END** of the infection.

START

END

Clean Your Plate

Would you like to enter a contest to eat as much pie or as many hot dogs as you can? Sounds good, but some eating contests are not as tasty. How about trying to eat the most pickled eggs, mayonnaise, or slimy green pods of boiled okra? Or, go to the World Eskimo Indian Olympics and try eating "muktuk" *(whale blubber)*. YUM!

GROSS, BUT TRUE!

Oleg Zhornitskiy holds the record for eating 16 cups of mayonnaise in 8 minutes. Takeru Kobayashi has the record for eating 17.7 pounds of cooked cow brains in 15 minutes. C. Manoharan slurped down 200 earthworms in 30 seconds. That's certainly a record!

Chomp your way through this eating contest.

Scorpion Soup

Many people would shriek if they saw a scorpion in their kitchen. But in some parts of the world scorpions are cooked into a tasty soup! Grab a spoon and see if you can find your way through this serving. Be careful not to eat the tips of the tails!

START

END

Cherry on Top

What kind of tree could grow a cherry as bright as the one you get on a hot fudge sundae? The answer is no tree on this planet! To make a maraschino cherry, a regular cherry has to be soaked in a lye solution until all the natural color and taste are bleached out. Then this white, flavorless, cherry-shaped glob of fruit is soaked in artificial color and sugar syrup. Oh yes, the cherries are also soaked in calcium chloride so they stay firm, not squishy!

START eating at the bottom of this sundae. Does your path **END** up going near any bleached cherries?

END

START

GROSS, BUT TRUE!

To make "agutuk," or native Alaskan ice cream, melt one pound of reindeer fat with two cups of seal oil. Mix with snow, and add wild berries.

Why Not Try Tripe?

A cow has four stomachs used to digest the grass and hay it eats. If you take the lining of the first three stomachs and eat it for dinner, you're having what is called tripe! Chefs have to clean the tripe very carefully. If any of the cow's last meal is left in the stomach, it will smell too gross to eat! *(But it seems that dogs really like their tripe this way . . .)*

Which stomach will this diner be ordering tonight? START eating to find out!

Tasty Termites

If you ever travel to Singapore, be careful what you eat for appetizers. A gourmet snack is a live termite queen *(2 inches or longer are the tastiest)*. Not sure about eating live termites? OK, travel to South Africa where you can get your termites fried in oil and served with tomato!

START with a termite and **END** with a quick bite!

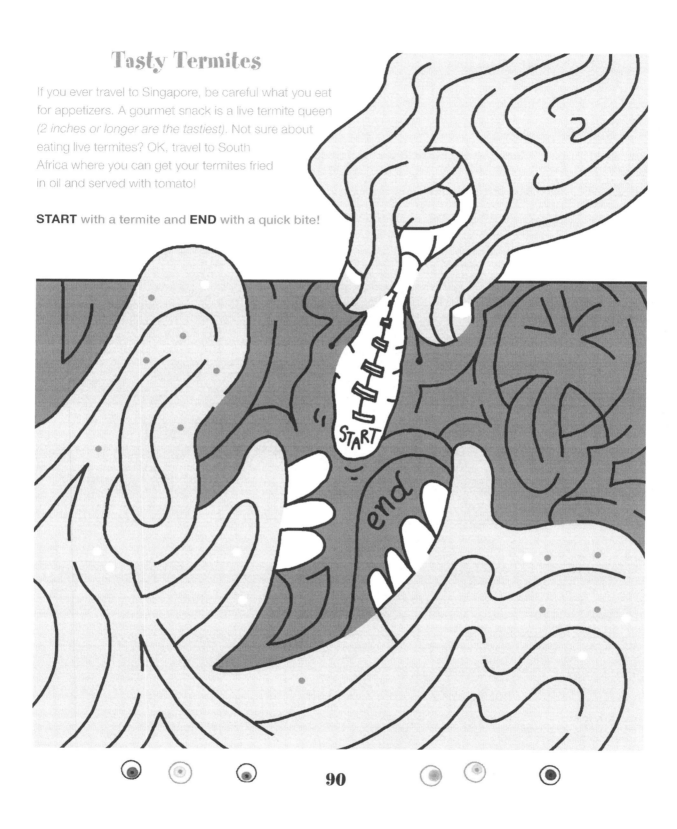

PBJ

Bees make honey, right? Well, bees also make another gooey substance that people eat. "Royal jelly" oozes out from special glands in the head of a worker bee. Workers use it to feed the baby bees, and even to turn a regular bee into a queen. People who eat royal jelly claim it is full of vitamins and minerals. But would you want to eat something scraped off the head of a bee?

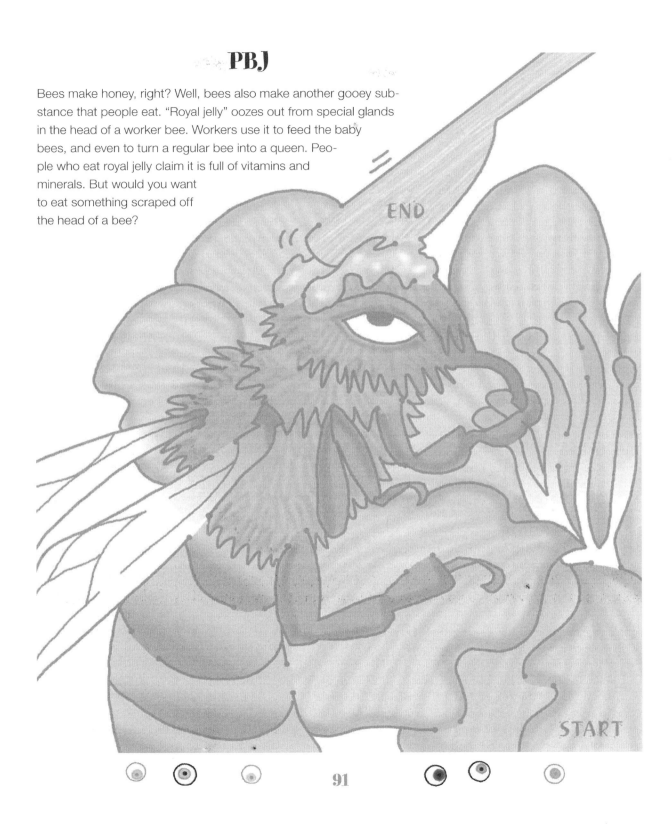

END

START

Fatal Fish

Almost every part of the Japanese pufferfish *(or fugu)* is extremely poisonous! It can be deadly to eat, and dangerous to even touch the skin, muscles, skeleton, intestines, or liver. In fact, the parts of the fugu that go in the trash are treated as toxic waste and must be thrown away at a special dump. Yet restaurants in Japan still serve fugu—even though about 100 people a year die from eating it!

START eating. Will you END up enjoying the meal?

Haggis Anyone?

Here's what you need to make this traditional Scottish favorite: heart of a sheep, plus the sheep's liver, windpipe, and lungs, onion, oatmeal, fat, and salt. Cut this all into little pieces, mix well, stuff it into the sheep's stomach, and boil for several hours. Yum!

PS: If you don't want to actually eat the haggis, you can bring it to the playing field and see how far you can toss it. World record? 180 feet, 10 inches for a 1½-pound haggis!

START eating your haggis.
Will you finish it? Or will
you END up tossing it?

Please Pass the Rotten Shark

Natives of Iceland celebrate their Viking heritage at a Thorrablot feast. The menu might include sheep's blood pudding, burned-then-boiled sheep head, and rotten shark meat—dug up and served after being buried for months! If that all sounds too gross to stomach, you can always eat just the "thunder bread," so called because it tends to make you fart!

PS: Don't try making your own rotten shark at home. You have to let it rot a certain way or it will make you sick!

START eating and see if you can taste everything before the feast ENDs!

Bird's Nest Soup?

Swiftlets are tiny birds that live in caves. Since there isn't any building material in a cave, swiftlets use their own gooey saliva to make their nests! As the bird spits out and shapes the strands of the nest, the saliva becomes tough and rubbery. In southeast Asia, many people enjoy eating soup made from these nests simmered in chicken broth. Is bird "spit" soup worth it? It had better be. Harvesters who climb into the caves to pry the nests from the rocks often fall to their deaths!

START cooking. Find the path that **END**s up going through all three bowls of soup.

Stinky Cheese

What do you do with moldy cheese? Throw it out?
Wait, some cheeses are *supposed* to be moldy!
It's weird to think that it would not be good if you
found these same molds growing in your basement.
What is even weirder is that some people like to eat
cheese that is squishy and covered with mold and
smells like an old basement!

Use Your Brains

Even cavemen knew that untreated animal hides would quickly rot and fall apart. People soon learned that rubbing something fatty into the hide was a good way to make long-lasting leather. What was the most popular fatty material? Raw brains! Other favorites were liver, sour milk, or raw egg yolk. Not gross enough? Some leathermakers soaked hides in urine to soften them up! *(Some leathermakers still do—would you?)*

START

END

Monster Movie Extra

A man runs through the night, chased by a gang of half-rotted zombies. Skin flapping, blood dripping, eyeballs hanging, covered with gore and intestines—good thing it's only makeup! In fact, some movie monsters sit for 5 or 6 hours while makeup artists get them looking perfectly awful. How would you like to be the person under all the rubber, fake blood, and slimy goop?

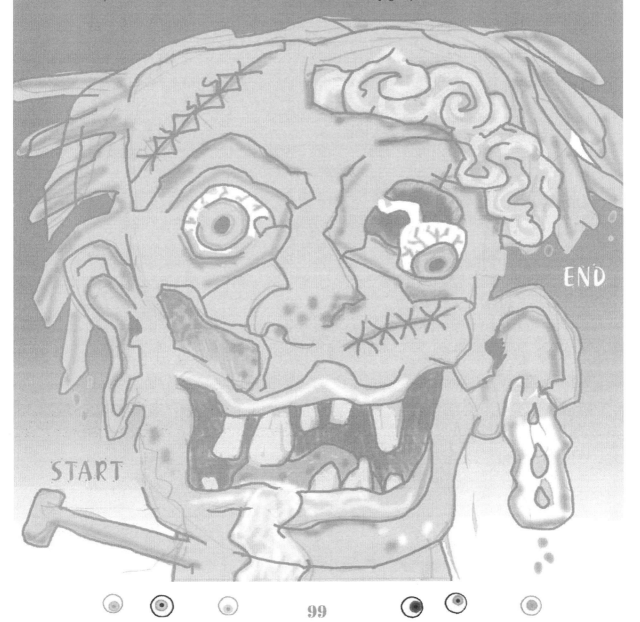

START

END

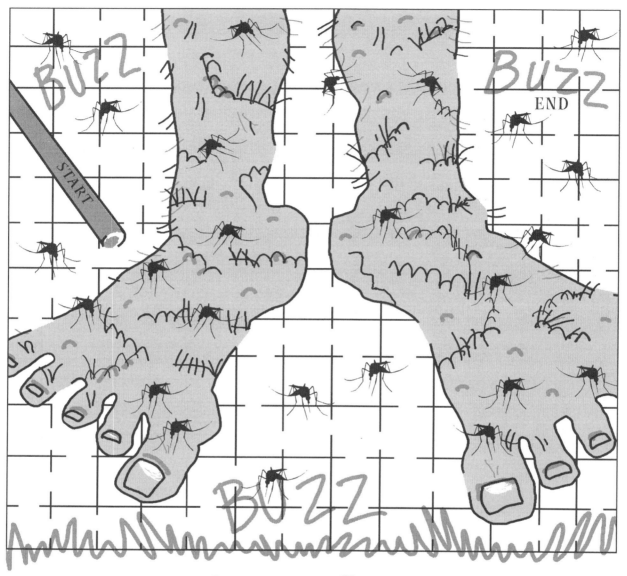

Mosquito Collector

Scientists who study how mosquitoes spread disease need to study live mosquitoes! The best way to do this is to have someone sit in a tent with a narrow opening near the ground. Mosquitoes get trapped inside and start to bite the collector on the ankles. Quickly, the collector uses his or her mouth to suck the mosquitoes into a big straw and puff them out into a container. On a good night several hundred mosquitoes can be captured this way! Would you like to get bitten for science?

   100

Airplane Cleaning Crew

Imagine you're on a really bumpy flight. The plane rocks back and forth, shoots straight up, and then drops down fast. Oh no, you've got to barf! Well, you and about two dozen other passengers. When you finally land and everyone staggers off the plane, do you take the barf bags home with you? Nope. You leave them for the cleaning crew.

Zooper Scooper

When you go to the zoo and look at all the animals, you don't often see piles of poop lying around. That's because someone on the zoo staff goes in and cleans the cages and pens. That's not too bad when the critters are tiny, but what about big animals like elephants or hippos? One hippo can make a hundred pounds of poop a night, and they like to splash it around, too! Any zoo scooping for you?

Food Tasters

Some people get paid to taste things! Usually the samples are nice, like soup or pizza. But what about the tasters who helped develop the currently popular "magical" assortment of jelly-beans that includes vomit, earwax, and booger flavors? Someone checked that they tasted like the real thing—would you?

See if you can find which flavor this taster will get next.

Start

ROTTEN EGG

Mothball

Turnip

Broccoli

FROG

Lint

Sour Milk

Haggis

Pencil

Tripe

Termite

Worm

Mushroom

Jellyfish

GARLIC

Sewer Diver

The poop, pee, and everything else from 20 million people all flow into the ancient sewer system of Mexico City, Mexico. The liquid that sloshes through the huge pipes is so murky and full of "stuff," even a spotlight can't cut through it. So what happens if a pipe gets backed up? A trained diver puts on a special diving suit, is lowered deep into the sewers, and feels his way through the sludge until he reaches the clog. What will he find . . . a bicycle, a basketball, or a dead body? Would you want to find out?

Fake Poop Maker

You've seen those disgusting piles of fake poop sold in joke shops or catalogs. Some stores even sell fake poop you can hide a house key inside. Well, someone goes to work every day to make those poops . . . mixing the plastic and dye to just the right color, squeezing it out to just the right shape. Hey, someone's gotta do the doo-doo! Would you?

start

END

Odor Judge

How does a mouthwash company know if its product works? First an odor judge has to sniff the mouth of someone with really stinky breath. This is the bad part. Then after Mr. or Ms. Badbreath uses the mouthwash, the judge sniffs again to see if the smell is better. This is the OK part, unless the mouthwash doesn't work! Would you turn up your nose at this job?

What if the company was trying to get rid of garlic breath?

Scatologist

If you want to study a wild animal, but that animal is hard to find, how can you get any info? Study its poop! The animal might be hiding, but no matter where it sneaks off to, it leaves piles of poop, or "scat." Scatologists are special scientists whose job it is to study poop. They can tell what an animal ate *(look for berries, seeds, or bones)*, if the animal is sick *(look for worms)*, or even if the animal is close or far away *(fresh poop or old dried-out poop)*. Think you'd like to scan some scat?

Gross Artist

There are almost 100 different mazes in this book. Look carefully, and you will see a LOT of gross drawings! There are rotten feet and rotten sharks, live termites being eaten, and dead mummies getting their brains pulled out, plus skin full of zits, and wiggly mites that live in the skin of your eyelids. Someone had to research all this gross stuff, look at two or three times the number of gross pictures you see here, and then create new and even more disgusting illustrations for you to enjoy. Would you like to do this?

Appendix 1

Look Again!

Just when you thought you had worked your way through all the puzzles, there's one more! See if you can find each of these picture pieces somewhere in this book. Write the name of the puzzle each piece is from in the space under each box.

1.

2.

3.

4.

5.

6.

7.

8.

9.

HINT: There is only one picture piece from each chapter.

Appendix 2
References

If you haven't had enough of gross stuff, there are plenty of books you can read or Web sites you can visit. Below are listed a few of our favorites.

Books

Kids' Bathroom Book of Mazes

By Sterling Publishing (2004). These short mazes are not about the bathroom, they are designed for doing while you are using the bathroom! The companion volume, *Kids' Bathroom Book of Weird Facts*, has some good gross reading. Both books are good fun even outside of the can!

Poop

By Nicola Davies, illustrated by Neal Layton (2004). Everything, and we do mean everything, you ever wanted to know about poop. Funny and informative, with great pictures that will keep you giggling even when you want to say "Eeeeew!"

Hands-On Grossology

By Sylvia Branzei, illustrated by Jack Keely (2003). Want to do more than just deal with grossness on the printed page? Here are over 30 experiments to let you get hands deep in gross. Includes a recipe for fake edible barf!

Mummies: The Newest, Coolest, and Creepiest from Around the World

By Shelly Tanaka (2005). A fascinating look at the creepy world of dead bodies that just won't go away. Caution: There are some very close-up and sometimes grisly pictures of mummies.

Ripleys' Believe It or Not! Special Edition 2006

By Ripley Entertainment (2005). Explore the bizarre, the amazing, and, of course, the gross with the latest collection from Ripley. Meet the man who wants to become a lizard, a woman who had her legs broken so she could grow taller, and a whole zoo full of animals with attitude.

Oh Yuck! The Encyclopedia of Everything Nasty

By Joy Masoff (2000). If you want to know "all the best stuff about some of the worst stuff on earth." then this is the book for you. From acne to eye gunk, fleas to feet, parasites to puking, it is all here.

Gross Universe: Your Guide to All Disgusting Things Under the Sun

By Jeff Szpirglas (2004). A guide to many of the disgusting, yet amazing, things in our world—be it animal, plant, or human.

Grossology series (1995–2004)

By Sylvia Branzei. A bestselling book series including the titles *Grossology and You, Animal Grossology, Hands-On Grossology,* and others. Lots of information on all things gross and disgusting combined with hands-on activities.

Nature's Yucky

By Lee Ann Landstrom (2003). Explores icky, but interesting, facts about the behavior of some animals—and the good reasons they have for what they do.

Web Sites

http://mazoons.com

Mazoons is a Maze/Cartoon Web site created and maintained by artist Jody Hall. There are step-by-step directions on how to make your own maze, plus free mazes to print out and enjoy. Check out the great collection of mazes sent in by kids like you!

www.pbrc.hawaii.edu/microangela/

The University of Hawaii has provided a whole gallery of colorized photos taken with their scanning electron microscope. Tiny mites, lice, roaches, mosquitoes, fleas, and other creepy crawlies are shown at huge magnification. You'll be able to see every gross and amazing detail!

www.poison-ivy.org

Go to this site and click on the link for the "Grody Poison Ivy-Oak Skin Rash Hall of Fame Slideshow." If you thought that poison ivy just caused a mild rash and a little bit of itching, you will think again! This slide show has over 40 seriously gross pictures of what poison ivy can actually do to human skin. Do *not* eat lunch before you look at these pics!

www.scienceman.com/pgs/
    archive21_owlpellet.html

This site gives you an incredibly detailed look at the bones found inside of an owl pellet! Click on any one of 10 different pictures to zoom right in.

http://oceanlink.island.net/oinfo/hagfish/
    hagfish.html

This site has some great gooey pictures of slimy hagfish.

http://oceanlink.island.net/oinfo/hagfish/
    hagfishathome.html

Some science students got a little crazy and tried baking scones using hagfish slime instead of eggs! Read what happened.

http://express.howstuffworks.com/
    bionic-body.htm

This site takes a detailed look at what parts of the human body can now be replaced.

www.guinnessworldrecords.com

Get lost here looking at the world records for strange diseases, incredible body parts, and medical marvels. Whether it is the champion eyeball popper, the longest sneezing bout, or the person who can spit a dead cricket the farthest, we guarantee you will be fascinated!

www.yucky.kids.discovery.com

This site declares itself the "Yuckiest Site on the Internet"! It contains lots of information on gross and cool body stuff, and has whole sections on worms and roaches. It also has a great fun and games area that is divided into things like creepy crafts, revolting recipes, and icky experiments.

www.grossology.org

The Web site of Sylvia Branzei and Jack Keely, author and illustrator of the *Grossology* series. Information on both individuals, a grossology store, and recipes for fake blood, barf, snot, and more!

page 2 • Tattoo Black & Blue

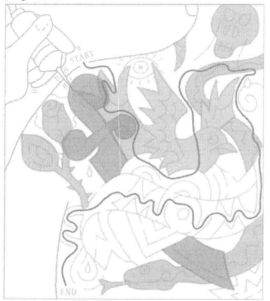

page 3 • Icky Itchy Ivy

page 4 • Wacky Warts

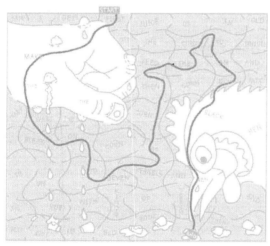

FIRST MAKE THE WART BLEED ON TO
SEVEN KERNELS OF CORN. THEN FEED
THE CORN TO AN OLD, BLACK HEN.

page 5 • Abandon Ship!

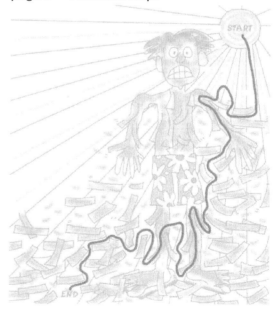

Puzzle Answers

page 6 • There's a Fungus among Us

page 7 • A Change of Face

page 8 • Zit, Zat, Zut

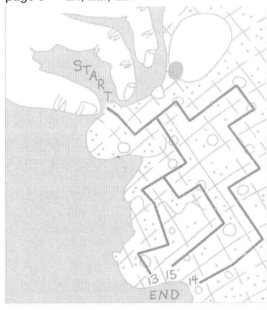

page 9 • Mud Bath

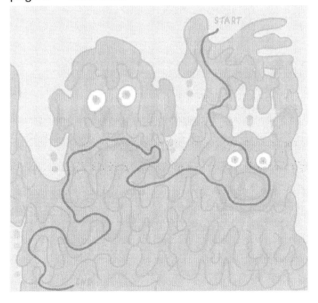

page 10 • Coming Through

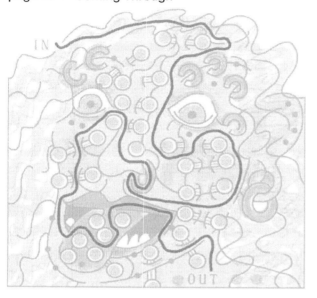

page 11 • Can't Stop Shedding

page 12 • Patches

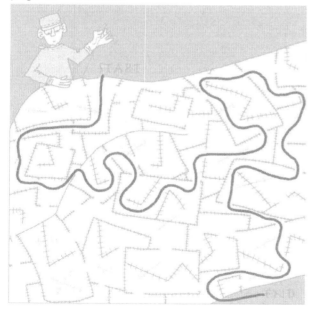

page 14 • Brain Drain

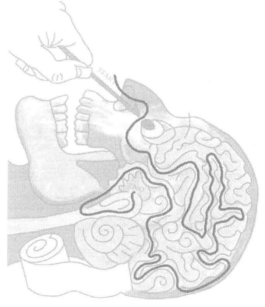

Puzzle Answers

page 15 • Modern Mummies

page 16 • Can I Have a T-shirt?

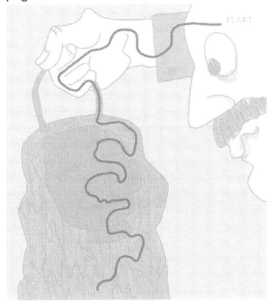

page 17 • Are You in There?

page 18 • Yummy Mummy?

The EVERYTHING KIDS' Gross Mazes Book

page 19 • No Vacancy

page 20 • Z-Z-Z-Zombies

page 21 • Crash Test Bodies?

page 22 • True or False

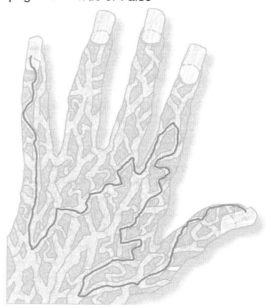

Puzzle Answers

page 23 • Lend a Hand

page 24 • Dead Men DO Tell Tales!

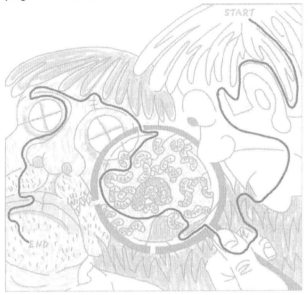

page 26 • S.S.S. (Shed Snake Skin)

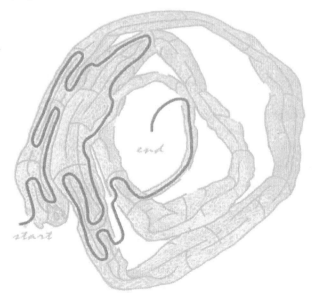

page 27 • H.D.C. (Hot Dog Casings)

page 28 • T.H. (Tomato Hornworms)

page 29 • B.B. (Beach Blobs)

page 30 • Y.D.V. (Yellow Dog Vomit)

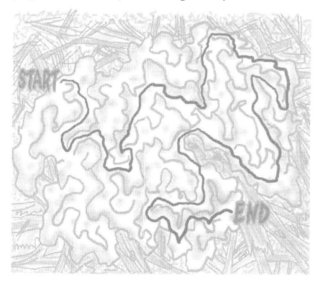

page 31 • E.T. (Exploding Toads)

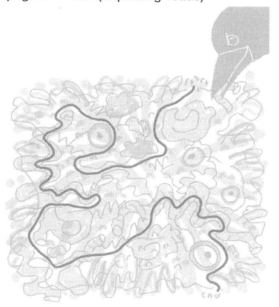

Puzzle Answers

page 32 • D.G. (Dugout Glop)

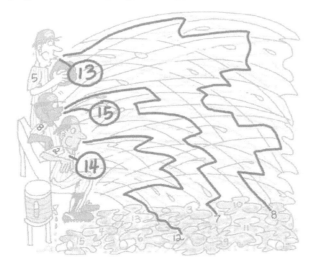

page 33 • F.F.B. (Forest Furballs)

page 34 • P.W.N. (Paper Wasp Nest)

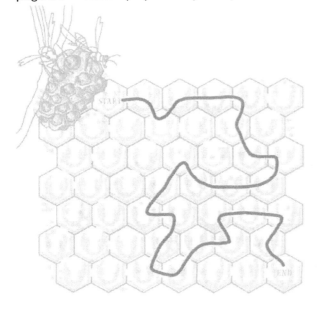

page 35 • F.W.B. (Floating White Blobs)

The EVERYTHING KIDS Gross Mazes Book

page 36 • U.D.C. (Under Desk Crunchies)

page 38 • Scraping Slime

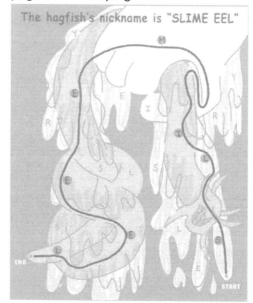

page 39 • Splat!

page 40 • Hard Water

Puzzle Answers

page 41 • Soapy Stew

page 42 • Clean Cats

page 43 • Next!

page 44 • Scoop the Poop!

page 45 • Can't Blink, Gotta Slurp!

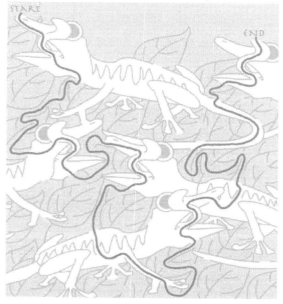

page 46 • Lid Down!

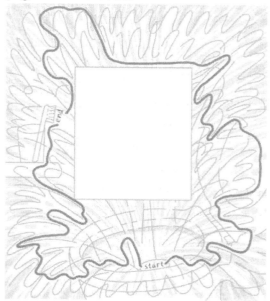

page 47 • Pass the Toothpaste

page 48 • Hair and Gone

Puzzle Answers

page 50 • Lose Your Lunch

page 51 • Space Toilet

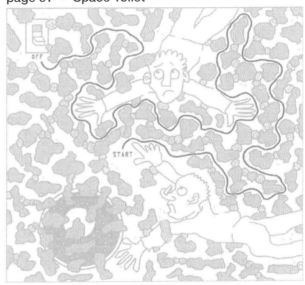

page 52 • Tooting Termites

page 53 • ACHOOO!

page 54 • Stand Back

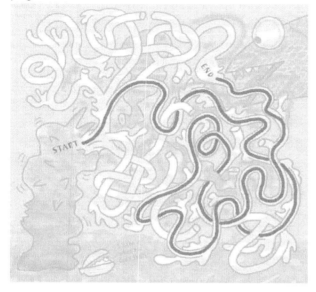

page 55 • Twice as Good

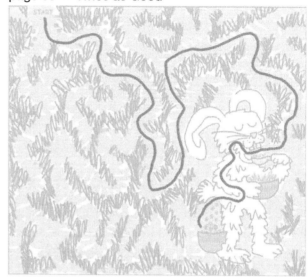

page 56 • Zip It Up

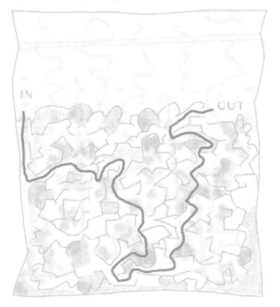

page 57 • Knock, Knock

Puzzle Answers

page 58 • Spew for Science

page 59 • Garbage In, Fertilizer Out

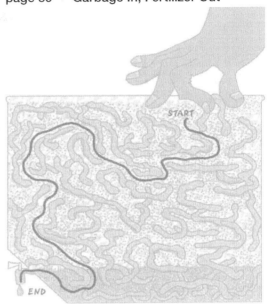

page 60 • HA HA!

page 62 • Terrible Teeth

page 63 • Jeepers, Creepers, Where'd You . . .

page 64 • Did You Lose This?

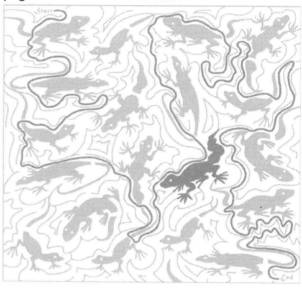

page 65 • I've Been Scalped!

page 66 • Fill in the Face

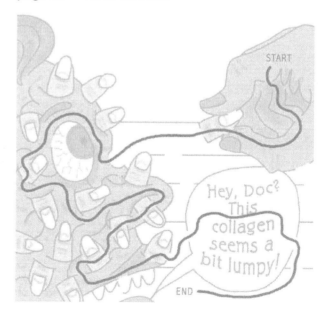

Puzzle Answers

page 67 • Why did the mad scientist grow . . .

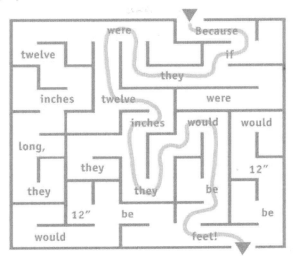

page 68 • Lost and Found

page 69 • Got Blood?

page 70 • How to Fix a Broken Heart

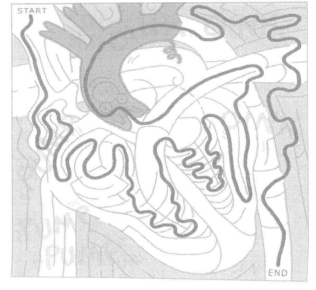

page 71 • It's Hip to Be Fake

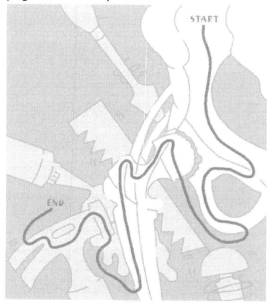

page 72 • I See You

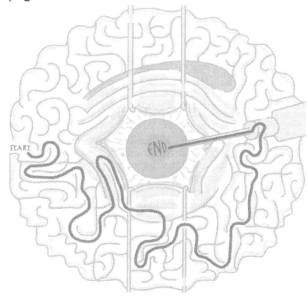

page 74 • Tainted Toothbrush

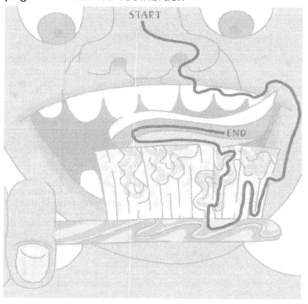

page 75 • Bzzzzz, SLAP!

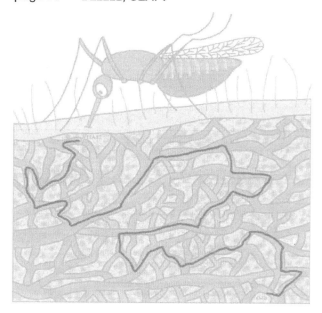

Puzzle Answers

page 76 • Feast for a Flea

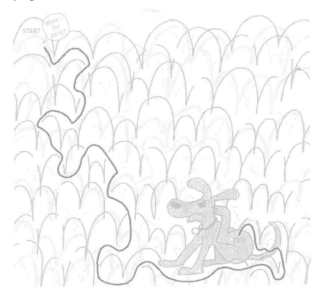

page 77 • Itchy Scratchy

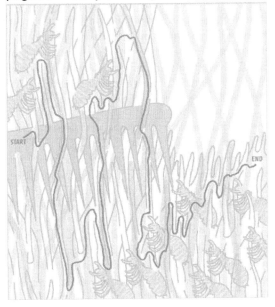

page 78 • Gotta Run

page 79 • Allergy Attack

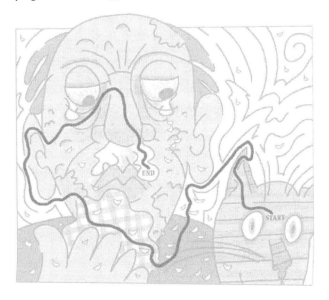

page 80 • ACHOO!

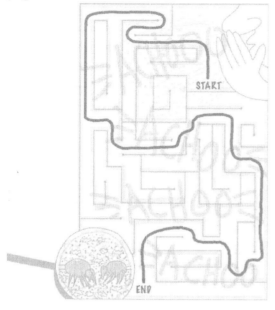

page 81 • They Live WHERE?

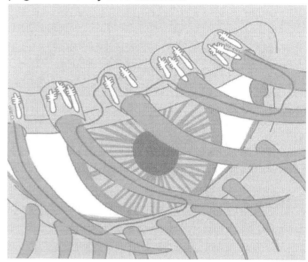

page 82 • I Vant Your Body Fluids

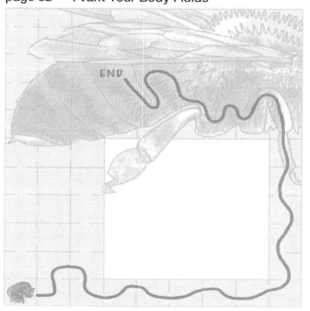

page 83 • Numerous Nematodes

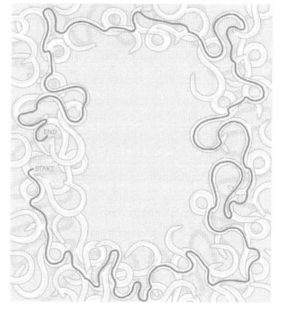

Puzzle Answers

page 84 • Flesh-Eating Bacteria

page 86 • Clean Your Plate

page 87 • Scorpion Soup

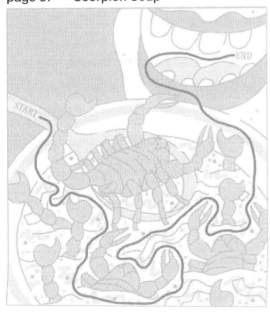

page 88 • Cherry on Top

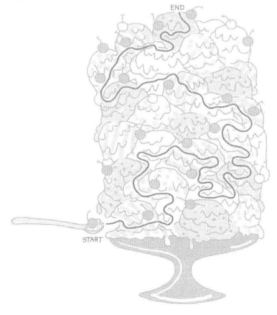

page 89 • Why Not Try Tripe?

page 90 • Tasty Termites

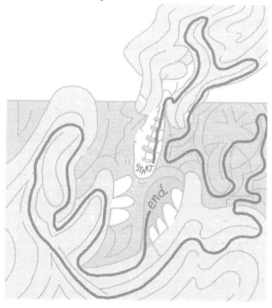

page 91 • PBJ

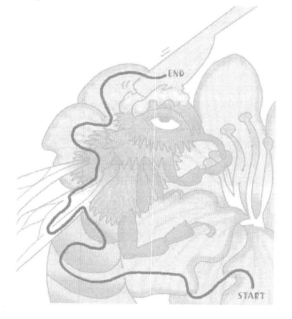

page 92 • Fatal Fish

Puzzle Answers

page 93 • Haggis Anyone?

page 94 • Please Pass the Rotten Shark

page 95 • Bird's Nest Soup?

page 96 • Stinky Cheese

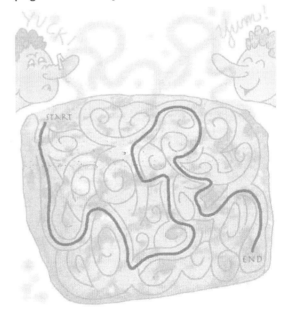

page 98 • Use Your Brains

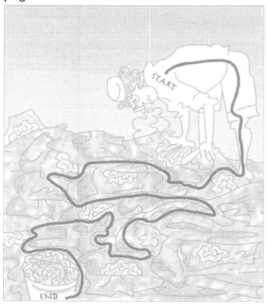

page 99 • Monster Movie Extra

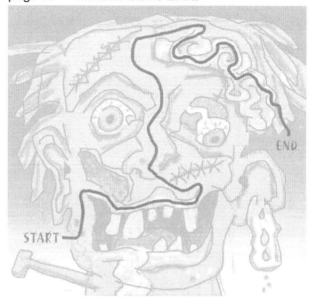

page 100 • Mosquito Collector

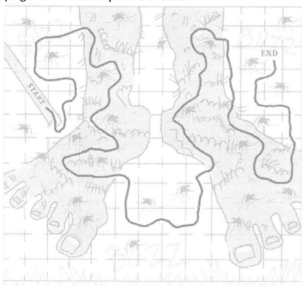

page 101 • Airplane Cleaning Crew

   134

Puzzle Answers

page 102 • Zooper Scooper

page 103 • Food Tasters

page 104 • Sewer Diver

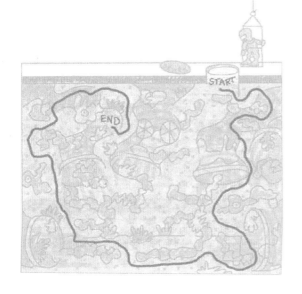

page 105 • Fake Poop Maker

page 106 • Odor Judge

page 107 • Scatologist

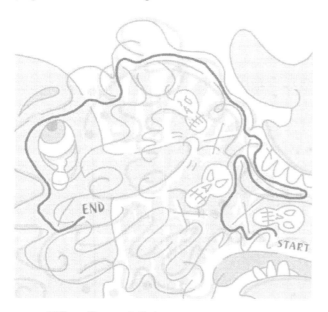

page 108 • Gross Artist

page 109 • Look Again!

1. Patches

2. Lend a Hand

3. F.W.B.

4. Hard Water

5. Stand Back

6. Jeepers Creepers

7. I Vant Your...

8. Stinky Cheese

9. Gross Artist

The Everything® Kids'
GROSS Series

Chock–full of sickening entertainment for hours of disgusting fun.

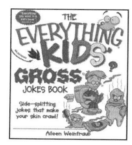

The Everything® Kids'
Gross Jokes Book
1-59337-448-8, $7.95

The Everything® Kids' Gross
Puzzle & Activity Book
1-59337-447-X, $7.95

The Everything® Kids'
Gross Mazes Book
1-59337-616-2, $7.95

The Everything® Kids' Gross
Hidden Pictures Book
1-59337-615-4, $7.95

Made in the USA
San Bernardino, CA
09 April 2014